THE LAST MESSAGE

The Lord is the True Author

A Prophetic Message by:

THE HOLY ONE

Edited by Ruth-Dow

Copyright © 2022 by Ruth-Dow.

ISBN   Softcover   978-1-950580-58-3
       Hardcover   978-1-950580-59-0
       eBook   978-1-950580-60-6

All rights reserved. No part of this book may be reproduced or transmitted in any form or by any means, electronic or mechanical, including photocopying, recording, or by any information storage and retrieval system without express written permission from the author, except in the case of brief quotations embodied in critical reviews and certain other non-commercial uses permitted by copyright law.

Printed in the United States of America.

To order additional copies of this book, contact:
Bookwhip
1-855-339-3589
https://www.bookwhip.com

CONTENTS

DEDICATION xi
INTRODUCTION xiii
PROLOGUE: The Messenger's Story xvii

CHAPTER 1. WHAT IS DELIVERANCE? 1
   TEACHING on THE IMPORTANCE of DELIVERANCE 1

CHAPTER 2. WHAT IS SALVATION? 2

CHAPTER 3. LESSONS FOR GROWTH 4
   TEACHING on THE FATHER, and THE TRINITY 4
   TEACHING on LESSONS TO BE PASSED ON 5
   TEACHING on "MY PRESENCE" 6
   TEACHING on "MY JUSTICE" 7
   TEACHING on THE IMPORTANCE of BAPTISM 9
   TEACHING on THE LORD SPEAKS MORE in
      SILENCE THAN in WORDS 9
   TEACHING on: "I TREAT MY CHILDREN with
      LOVE and TENDERNESS" 10
   TEACHING on OBEDIENCE and TRUST 10
   TEACHING on LETTING the HURT CHILD GO, and
      GROWING UP! 11
   TEACHING on LOVE YOURSELF; THEN YOU CAN
      LOVE OTHERS 12
   TEACHING on GIVING, and HELPING A STRANGER 12
   TEACHING on DREAMS 13
   TEACHING on CELEBRATING THE LORD'S LOVE
      on ST. VALENTINE'S DAY 14
   TEACHING on CELEBRATING FATHER'S DAY 14

TEACHING on THE FATHER'S LOVE 15
TEACHING on PATIENCE 15
*TEACHING on SHOWERING with LOVE,
    KINDNESS and PEACE* 16
TEACHING on GIVING THE LORD the GLORY 17
TEACHING on REMAINING TRUE to YOUR HEART 17

CHAPTER 4. WHY SEEK ME? 18
TEACHING on COMPOSITION OF PRAYER 18
TEACHING on: "TIME SPENT with ME!" 19
TEACHING on TIME MANAGEMENT 21
TEACHING on PROTECTING YOUR HEART 22
TEACHING on MONEY 22
*TEACHING on: "THE LORD SPEAKS THE
    LANGUAGE OF MUSIC"* 23
*TEACHING on "ONE-ON-ONE - THE FULL
    CYCLE OF LOVE"* 25
TEACHING on RAYS OF THE SUN: 25
TEACHING on PASCHAL PRAYER FOR THE DECEASED ... 26

CHAPTER 5. TEMPTATIONS, TRIALS AND
    TRIBULATIONS 27
TEACHING on "YOU MUST CHOOSE ME FIRST!" 27
TEACHING on WORDS OF WISDOM 29
*TEACHING on "SPREAD YOUR WINGS,
    and FLY OVER the FOG!"* 30
TEACHING on CLEANSING 31
TEACHING on FAITH IS KEY! 31
TEACHING on LISTENING CAREFULLY! 32
TEACHING on FOCUS 34

TEACHING on "THE BRIDGE" - HOW TO FLEE
    TEMPTATION, and HOW TO STAY FOCUSED
    on THE LORD 35
TEACHING on POSITIVITY..39
TEACHING on DISOBEDIENCE and REPENTANCE..........41
TEACHING on RESILIENCY: REPETITION and
    RESISTANCE..43
TEACHING on THE HEART and FAITH 48
TEACHING on GOSSIPPING..49
TEACHING on POSITIVE THINKING 49
TEACHING on THE TIMING TO SPEAK.............................53
TEACHING on RIDDLES, RIDDLES, RIDDLES..................53
TEACHING on SILENCE..55
TEACHING on THE BURNING FIRE of RAGE!...................56
TEACHING on UNITY, STRENGTH and FAITH 57
TEACHING on REFLECTIONS..60
TEACHING on TIME IS TICKING FOR YOU......................62
TEACHING on DEMONIC OPPRESSION,
    AND SELF-PUNISHMENT 62
TEACHING on OUR WILL.. 64
TEACHING on "YOU REAP WHAT YOU SOW"..................65
TEACHING on FAITH and OBEDIENCE 65
TEACHING on "MY LOVE HAS FILLED YOUR HEART"...66
TEACHING on JESUS' LOVE 69
TEACHING on AVOIDING TEMPTATION ALTOGETHER....71
TEACHING on "I GIVE IN BLESSING, and TAKE
    AWAY IN FURY!"..71
TEACHING on A SEASON FOR EVERY TIME....................72
TEACHING on REMAINING SWEET BUT THIRSTY 72
TEACHING on "I HEAR YOU SPEAK!" 73
TEACHING on RETALIATION: AS CRUEL AS REVENGE!....74

TEACHING on DISCIPLINE TO MAINTAIN OBEDIENCE ...75
TEACHING on KEYS TO GRATITUDE ...76
TEACHING on A PEACEFUL MIND ...81
TEACHING on THE LORD'S TIREDNESS! ...81
TEACHING on "I AM HERE, WAITING FOR YOU TO COME MY WAY!" ...83
TEACHING on "THE LORD COMES! GET READY FOR MY WORK!" ...85
TEACHING on BELIEVE! EVERYTHING IS POSSIBLE, and NOTHING IS IMPOSSIBLE! ...86
TEACHING on "I AM HERE!" ...88
TEACHING on "THE FATHER HAS GRANTED YOUR WISH!" ...89
TEACHING on SELF-WORTH ...91
TEACHING on "CELEBRATE, and BE JOYFUL IN PRAISE!" ...94
TEACHING on THE LORD'S REASSURANCE ...95

CHAPTER 6. ALL THE GIFTS ...99
TEACHING on THE GIFTS of MANDATORY SILENCE ...99
TEACHING on COMMUNICATION with "THE FATHER!" ...105
TEACHING on THE ULTIMATE GIFT on GOOD FRIDAY: "WE ARE ONE, I AM HER!" ...106
TEACHING on THE GIFTS of HOLINESS and COMMUNION ...107
TEACHING on "THE GIFTS of MY BLOOD and BREATH" ...107
TEACHING on CLAIMING GIFTS ...109
TEACHING on THE GIFTS of FEEDING YOU MY WORD, WISDOM, COURAGE and STRENGTH ...111
TEACHING on THE GIFT of MY SWORD ...111

TEACHING on THE GIFT of BURNING RODS 112
*TEACHING on GIFTS of THE BIRD OF FREEDOM,
  and THE WATER OF LIFE* 112
TEACHING on THE GIFT of THE HEALING SPIRIT 112
*TEACHING on THE GIFT of FRIENDSHIPS IN
  UNITY WITH THE LORD* 113
*TEACHING on THE GIFTS of MY GRAPES, MY
  SCROLL and ASHES FOR JOY* 114
*TEACHING in "NO ONE CAN GIVE GIFTS EXCEPT
  FOR US"* 114

CHAPTER 7. MINISTRY 115
TEACHING on THE LORD's PROMISES COME IN 7 x 77! ... 115
TEACHING on CIRCLES 116
TEACHING on LISTENING to MY WISE WORDS 117

CHAPTER 8. CHOICES 120
TEACHING on "CHOOSE ME!" 120

CHAPTER 9. MANDATES TO SPIRITUAL LIFE 124
TEACHING on "FEAR NOT DELIVERANCE!" 124
*TEACHING on CLEANING UP THROUGH
  DELIVERANCE* 125
TEACHING on EXPECT the UNEXPECTED 127
TEACHING on OBEDIENCE and TRUST 128
TEACHING on SPIRITUAL GIFTS 129
*TEACHING on THE GIFTS of a SINGING VOICE
  and of TONGUES* 129
TEACHING on "CHOOSE ME - TO DO MY WORK!" 130
TEACHING on WAKE UP! WAKE UP! WAKE UP! 132
TEACHING on COMFORT 135
TEACHING on FREE WILL 138

TEACHING on OUTCOMES 140
TEACHING on MATURITY 142
TEACHING on "YOU HAVE TURNED YOUR
    BACK ON ME!" 143
TEACHING on THE SALVATION of OTHERS 145
TEACHING on "CHECK THE HEART!" 146
TEACHING on FOLLOWING and LISTENING 147
TEACHING on BEING GRATEFUL and SEEKING
    PERFECTION 147
TEACHING on UNITY and STRENGTH;
    FORGIVENESS and LOVE 148
TEACHING on TIME IS RUNNING OUT! 149
TEACHING on THE LORD'S PRESENCE DURING
    SUFFERING and ABUSE 150
TEACHING on "LEAD THE SUFFERING TO MY
    THORNS!" 150
TEACHING on JUDGING OTHERS and ABSOLUTION ... 150
TEACHING on JUSTICE 151
TEACHING on SIMPLIFYING YOUR LIFE 151
TEACHING on PRAYER, WATERING THE FIELDS
    and PROTECTING THE HEART 151
TEACHING on "YOUR ONLY PERSONAL
    OBLIGATION IS TO ME!" 152
TEACHING on EQUAL PARTS LOVE, and EQUAL
    PARTS DISCIPLINE 153
TEACHING on SHARING YOUR FOOD:
    SOWING LOVE AND CARE (Ecclesiastes 11) 153
TEACHING on THE PROMISED MIRACLE 154
TEACHING on SHARING THE LORD'S BLESSINGS 155
TEACHING on MARRIAGE (1 Corinthians 7) 155
TEACHING on WOMEN'S HEAD COVERINGS:
    (1 Corinthians 11) 158

TEACHING on GIVING 158
TEACHING on TITHES and OFFERINGS 158
TEACHING on "THE CONFESSIONS OF
  SAINT AUGUSTINE" 159
TEACHING on "THE VULNERABLE ARE OPEN
  TO ALL STIMULI" 159
TEACHING on PROMISES 159
TEACHING on THE GOLDEN, ROYAL SHIELD
  of LIGHT 160

Prince of Peace
THE HOLY ONE

DEDICATION

"I declare to the nations how I work through people: how I heal people, how MY Spirit goes through and manifests; and how I protect, deliver, and live through My Children. 'The Last Message' reveals how I speak, how I discipline, and how I teach. It also reveals My Love and Patience, and how they endure above all.

"I AM a loving and patient God. I AM tender and gentle. I AM all-encompassing and glorying! But My People do not know who I AM! They do not know Me!

"They have not spent the time to know Me, and they still are lost among the masses like a sea full of sand!"

THE HOLY ONE

INTRODUCTION

"*When 'THE HOLY ONE' Speaks*"

"'The Holy One' is a term I use to identify Myself as The Lord, The Creator and The Almighty. I created all things in Heaven and earth, and it is through My thoughts that everything has been created. I choose to speak slowly and very deliberately, because it is the only way you will learn to speak as well: slowly and steadily. Everything has to be thought out very carefully, because that is how mistakes are avoided.

"Communicating with 'The Holy One' is very important. I AM the One, the Only, the Everlasting, the Eternal: in One! To communicate with Me is to keep in close proximity with Me. It is to feel My warmth, to feel My peace, to feel My joy, to feel My forgiveness! I AM the One Person you can share everything with, by choice. Yes, I already know what you are thinking, and what is to come; but by you sharing with Me, we form a union: a relationship that binds us stronger and tighter!

"It is essential for My People to learn to communicate with Me constantly, to thank Me for everything that happens: for beautiful weather, to beautiful clothing, to beautiful moments in their lives. It is important for My People to thank Me during sadness, hurt and all negative situations; for it is in those situations that they learn to turn to Me and trust Me, to lean on My strength *and support. For it is not the help they seek, but knowing they are taken care of that comforts their hearts.*

"My Children need to share their hearts' desires with Me in full detail: their daily events, the best and worst parts of their day, their trials and tribulations, their joys and thanksgivings. It will fortify our union, and break the ropes of bondage with the enemy.

"I need My People to realize that it is not too late, and that they can reach out to Me, especially during their joyous moments; because I share their joy and their desires. I gave My One and Only Son up for My People! My One and Only Son was tortured and crucified so My People could return home to their Father. But all I have gotten is heartache and anguish! The time is coming when they will not be able to repent if they do not change their ways, and turn to Me!

"Ways to communicate with Me are:

- *Speak to Me directly (vocally);*
- *Write to Me (in a manuscript or journal);*
- *Think of Me;*
- *Listen to My songs;*
- *Read My Holy Book;*
- *Have My Body and Blood;*
- *Pray to Me;*
- *Rejoice in My Presence in you: sing, dance and celebrate our dwelling together, as would a man and wife in their first home;*
- *Rejoice in all My gifts to My People; and cherish everything, never forgetting Me in the moment;*
- *Lie down with Me;*
- *Read to Me;*
- *Play music for Me (instruments);*
- *Thank Me for your pets, and your love;*
- *Speak to your mother and father;*

- *Speak to the hungry and cold;*
- *Bless your enemy, bless your foe.*

"Bless the Holy Spirit, and rejoice in His Power. There are many more ways to communicate with Me, but this is a start. Do not take this gift for granted! Do not take this luxury for granted! For there will come a time when you will not have the opportunity to speak to Me! I AM the ONLY Wisdom! Seek Wisdom in Me!

"Let us pray:

> 'My Lord in Heaven, Creator of Heaven and earth, Ruler of Heaven and earth: Your Will, Your Voice echoes for centuries; Your guidance and Wisdom is cried out by many! May Your People hear Your Words, and feel Your Spirit as times get harder and stronger.
>
> 'May My People hear My Voice, and help pass all evil temptation; for the sins of their past and choosing have dirtied their robes of glory. May they learn to forgive others as I AM forgiving them; may their hearts open to Me, as I open Myself to them; and may they be cleansed and delivered from now until My Coming - for My Breath and Spirit shall live on forever and ever through My Son, Jesus Christ, and the glory of My Love. Amen.'"

"The Holy One"

PROLOGUE:
THE MESSENGER'S STORY

"As a normal-appearing, pretty, university-educated woman in my twenties, I had enjoyed a relatively privileged life. However, everything began to unravel as I became progressively controlled and oppressed by satan and his demons. I was very disturbed and tormented by 'gifts of divination', which included fatalistic, gory premonitions.

"Four or five years earlier, a mutual friend introduced me to Ruth when I attended a Small-Group Meeting in her home. They were so committed to living for The Lord, that I was really impressed! I kept in touch with Ruth, and shared my problems with her; she would pray with me, and point me to Jesus. Due to my various trials, sometimes a month would pass before I would be in contact with her or anyone else: I was in 'escape-mode' because I couldn't face being around people.

"Suffocating in every aspect of my life: financial, career, familial, social and physical; I had been exposed to psychic phenomenon. I was in school full-time, and working full-time, making a minimum of $50,000.00 annually; however, this did not cover all my expenses. I prayed every night, based on the Biblical promises: 'Ask and you will receive, seek and you will find, knock and the door will be opened'.

"I asked The Lord to give me a new job which provided flexibility of time and oversight; was in a relaxing environment; and would come to me! The Lord provided the exact job I had requested! Now I knew there was a God who loved me, and that He listened to me.

"My parents were very severe, harsh, even abusive in their manner of expression and discipline, especially when I was a young child. Although I believed they loved me, I became very insecure. They both became sick; and as the only child, with no extended family, I was the sole provider.

"Weight was my biggest issue; for every success and failure, food became the constant means of reward and punishment. Having tried every diet imaginable, even to self-starvation on a fifty-five-day water fast which destroyed my metabolism, even basic water literally became poison to my system!

"During this period, I was closely in touch with Ruth, and we often prayed together. Marriage was a heavy topic since I was getting older. At my work place, however, there was a handsome young Muslim man who showed an interest in me. This was a great temptation to compromise my religion. After extensive prayer, I had the grace to choose The Lord Jesus over everything that the relationship could potentially offer. Again, Jesus answered my prayers!

"Immediately afterward, I met someone on-line. He sounded like he had a strong commitment with The Lord; however, when we met, it was clear that my commitment was far stronger. He was very bitter as a result of losing his parents, and was not interested in learning more about The Lord. The following day, I received closure with the man; more important, I found comfort and answers from The Lord!

"The third opportunity and test I endured within a period of three-to-four weeks was, again, regarding my greatest desire: to be married and have a family. I met another person who embodied every characteristic on my check-list, except he was not a committed Christian. Only on special occasions was he interested in attending Church. After praying that The Lord would not allow further pains of rejection, the man just disappeared!

"I learned that Ruth prayed for deliverance from demonic strongholds of oppression and bondage. Her prayers had helped draw me to Jesus, so I *joined her for special prayers. When I first saw the manifestation of demons being driven out by The Name of Christ Jesus, I was thoroughly freaked; the horror movies I had formerly enjoyed began to represent a frightening truth! As a matter of fact, at the first deliverance-prayer session I attended, I ended up sitting behind Ruth, watching the process from a safe distance, when I was supposed to be praying with her!*

"When Ruth and I began prayers for my deliverance, the first manifestation of the enemy was an unclean spirit named 'Ra', meaning 'chaos': a demon of divination! The master of many unclean spirits, 'Ra' refused to leave but began to relinquish demons under his control. Over a period of several months, I received deliverance from many evil spirits of rejection, fear-of-rejection, self-rejection, rebellion, anger, and roots of bitterness. The Lord was assisted by Saint Mary, His Mother, during many of these sessions! The demons would pitifully plead, even to requesting a transfer of allegiance back to The Lord; then they would fight and threaten in order to avoid returning to the pit!

"Early the next morning, I experienced extremely painful cramps in my abdomen. I shared with Ruth that, as I prayed for The Lord's help, the name 'Kyrie' kept coming into my mind. When 'Ra' was cast out with tortured cries, we offered thanksgiving and praise to The Lord; however, satan himself then manifested! He was ferocious, and told us that he had made a pact with 'Ra', who had impregnated me with 'Kyrie', in order to avoid being sent back to 'the pit'! If 'Kyrie' didn't succeed in her 'job', she was threatened to be skinned alive.

"In my spirit, I sensed that something 'big' was about to occur, so I warned Ruth. She quickly moved back all the furniture and ornamentation. At that point, the Spirit of The Lord began to slowly and powerfully pray through me 'The Lord's Prayer!' At the end, He loudly intoned and repeated three times: '. . . DELIVER US FROM ALL EVIL'!!! Involuntarily, I slid off the couch onto the floor, experiencing excruciating pain in my abdomen. I also cried because of the burning sensations in my hands! Believing that the heat and pain in my hands was associated with The Lord's wounds,

Ruth instructed me to put them on my abdomen; and I screamed out my deliverance from the demon 'Kyrie'. Again, The Lord Himself had delivered me!

"At this point, The Lord began to speak through me prophetically! Informing us that He had totally delivered me from satan and his demons, The Lord told us that He had chosen and gifted me to be His Healer and Messenger! He also warned that if anyone would not believe His Prophecies through me, they would perish."

Messenger (Name withheld for privacy).

CHAPTER 1

WHAT IS DELIVERANCE?

TEACHING on THE IMPORTANCE of DELIVERANCE

"You, Child, were spiraling down fast. If you continued on that path, you would eventually be destroyed. Would you have been able to go on much longer if you had not sought freedom? Your plea to return to Me is how you were set free. You had complete faith to CHOOSE ME and be My Servant!!! Otherwise, you would have succumbed to the enemy!

"When you fail, or are tempted, or filled with the enemy, your spirit too is filled, covered and struggling to breathe! You can use this to explain, in the future, what it is to be filled with the enemy, to require deliverance and truly how ugly the enemy really is! I will fill every hole the enemy leaves behind. The more cleansed you are, the emptiness I fill! The more full you become of My Spirit, the more joyous you feel!"

CHAPTER 2

WHAT IS SALVATION?

"Eternal Security is Salvation, but only I can give Eternal Security! For when you die, I will judge; and Security will be Mine to give - only when you die, and only when judgment day comes! The ONLY Eternal Security is death, spiritual death! When you die to self, you give Me power; when your body dies, your spirit is glorified. But Eternal Security is only attained when your spirit dies, and you become illuminated in My Glory!

"Death is not humanistic: when Jesus rose, His Spirit died. His Spirit died, for His Body left Him, and He became One with Me! Let Me explain. When you die, your body perishes; for it is just dirt. When you die, your spirit rises; but it is I Who decide whether the gates will open or shut! Your spirit must go through judgment; and that is when your spirit will either live illuminated in My Glory as a NEW spirit, or will perish, and die, and be tormented.

"Child, let Me explain in simple terms. When your pet bird fails and upsets you, what do you do? You discipline and yell at it, right? Well, when that pet is kissing you while you are angry at it, what do you do? You kiss it back, right? When you love that soul, you will do everything in your power to save it!

"Now, let us look at it in a different way. That pet becomes evil, bites and torments and makes all the other animals bleed! What will happen? Will you put it down, or will you allow it to torment others and itself? The soul of that bird will be saved or destroyed. Who makes that judgment is what will decide if the soul is saved or destroyed. For a pure soul with many faults will have a chance for illumination and glory, but a rotten soul will be damned!"

+++

"BLIND FAITH is the path to My Salvation. Blind Faith! Faith is the only attachment that can break all holds with the enemy! Choose Me!!! Without faith, your soul is empty, dark and shallow. With faith, it is a shining, brilliant jewel!"

+++

"It will not be easy to lose the people around you, as you have; but there will be more that will go. You will understand: they have many chances, Child. And even though you pray for Me to save them for you, it is not My Choice but theirs!"

CHAPTER 3

LESSONS FOR GROWTH

TEACHING on THE FATHER, and THE TRINITY

"Why do you describe The Father so harshly? Don't you realize He has endured all the pain and suffering from all humanity? He has seen His precious seeds perish, and He cannot do a thing about it! Child, let Me describe The Father:

- He is gentle, for He comes into you, and you do not feel any pain; for He is smooth and calm, so you do not feel fear. He is kind and loving, for He repeats your name like a song, over and over again. And He is sensitive, for He will treat you with kindness, as a mother caresses a baby;
- The Father is majestic. He is all-powerful, and He is King of all Kings! Remember that, when He enters you. He is ALL and EVERYTHING entering a small, restricted, controlled body that still has to maintain its free will to allow for anything to be said and done! So when you say He is scary, you are actually diminishing His Power and Glory! Fear is not God! Fear is evil!
- The Father is a loving Lord, sensitive and glorious! The next time He says your name, realize how small a voice you have; and how small He has to be, to be able to speak through you!

"So how do you explain The Father as MY FATHER? He is all-powerful, sensitive, loving, gentle, considerate and finally fulfilling."

+++

"We, the Trinity, are Three; but we are One! We are Three, but we are One! In a rainbow, there are seven colours; but together they form a rainbow of beauty. In Our Trinity, there are Three; but together they form One! I AM the Flesh: I AM the One that felt the pain, the anger, the hurt and the love. The Father is ONE: the Almighty, the all-knowing King of all kings. The Spirit is the Freedom: the flowy, the innocent, and the choice. Together, We form One! Everyone has the Spirit, but what they choose to do is freedom; what they choose to say is freedom. The Spirit is flowy, and all-encompassing.

"The soul is the only part of you to make choices; the soul is what the devil holds onto. The spirit is the replica of My Breath: I made you in My Image with My Breath. The Holy Spirit is where I reside in you. The Holy Spirit is Who provides the teaching of Wisdom. The Father, The Son and The Holy Spirit are One; all Three have existed simultaneously. All Three are Me! My Child, this is not for you to understand, but to live in by faith."

TEACHING on LESSONS TO BE PASSED ON

"My Child, My Words are lessons to be passed on: your life is a big lesson to be passed on! Your experience, and how you handle everything around you, is a lesson to be shared and cultivated. It is how you will grow, and how you will bless others through all your difficulties, whether financial, ethical, familial or psychological.

"You ask, 'Why'? The response is because it is The Father's Will to use you: to show others how you can change your life and shine! But at the same time, how you can fall, and be broken; and how you can crumble if you are not living in faith! Obedience, love, honour, praise, thanksgiving and faith are the core necessities to live a happy, fruitful and healthy life. Can you say you are obedient? Can you say you have love, and that you love The Father? What about Honour? Do you Honour the Lord: do you follow His Commandments, His Rules? Do you praise Him in all situations? Are you grateful to have Him in your life? All these questions, if answered with a 'YES' will lead you to a happy, healthy, and fulfilling life. Next time you wonder, 'Why?' ask yourself these questions, and see how your answer will reflect your attitude and emotions.

"Remember, even when The Lord gives warnings, you have a choice to make: to either follow, or to follow your own selfish heart. This statement will be a big stand you will carry with you! It can have the effect to change many lives, or to destroy! Make a decision on how you choose to use it, understand it, share it, and teach it. You were a great example. You had the knowledge, but you chose to follow your desires. With remorse you came back, but what you learned is significant. For you understood that The Lord's Word is the only TRUE Word!

"You have a great deal of work to do! You are chosen to do MY Work, an extension of My Arm! I would rather utilize My Instruments in you for deliverance. Do not worry! Just keep Me present; choose Me! Choose Me, and I will deliver all you seek. Choosing Me entails trusting Me, and allowing Me to rule! I see all, you see NONE! I SEE ALL, you see NONE! I can only protect you if you are Mine, Child! I have personally chosen you. You are My Servant and My Voice! I will continue to carry you for all the days of your life. I will continue to walk for you, breathe for you, and speak for you!"

<u>TEACHING on "MY PRESENCE"</u>

"My Child, I AM always here! I have told you that from the minute you close your eyes to sleep, to the minute you go back to sleep, I AM constantly with you, and with all My Children. You are always in My Presence: always! I watch you throughout the day and night. I have never left you!"

TEACHING on "MY JUSTICE"

"WHY ARE MY PEOPLE HURTING ME so dearly? I do not understand why they turn their backs on the one event, the thing that can possibly save their damned souls! THIS is why I have called My People to work for Me, to carry out My Work - for foolish hearts are broken! I suffer every time My Children fall! Every time they fall, I AM being nailed, I AM being whipped, and I AM being hung! My Heart hurts! My Tears are made of every Drop of Blood I shed! My People! My People! Why do they hurt Me so?

"Remember how justice was served in the past? The time is coming for Me to go to The Father again for justice! Justice will be served! The time is coming! My Child, this is why I have called you to work MY WORK!

"I told you tonight your choices would have huge implications! THIS is how they start! You decided to come out with ME, instead of going out for your pleasure; and in choosing Me, the enemy has caused a ploy to attack. Damned be their souls! Damned! Anger and Justice! The only way for them to be saved now is repentance and severe, severe judgment! Justice is a beautiful thing! The last time justice was served, there was protection. This time, there will be no protection!

"My People are select and few! I AM here! My Children, as long as I have people like you, My Work will carry on; but My Suffering is constant! For every second, there are Children falling - screaming and falling; and it is already too late! Yesterday was a day of joy!

THE LAST MESSAGE

Today is a day of joy for there are still people like My Chosen Ones out there. As long as there are My Chosen Ones, there is Hope!

"My Heart breaks! BREEAAAKKS!!! HUGE implications! If you, My Child, had chosen to go out to the outing, then the truth would not have been revealed! They plot to destroy what I have built! They plot to destroy My Work! Justice will be served! Justice will be served! I HAVE TRIED SO LONG TO BRING MY PEOPLE TO ME!!! MY HEART ACHES! THEY HAVE A CHOICE, AND THEY CHOOSE TO FALL - and leave what I have built for them!

"I promised to never destroy My People for the fall of one person! I will not destroy now, for the time is very quick - for distance is already here! There is no difference from the moment they hung MY SON to what they are doing now! They hung HIM because of sin! They hung HIM because of power and hunger! They hung HIM because of unbelief!!! Haven't I proved Myself to My People, for them to still continue to turn away and chose HIM, the most ugliest of them all???!!!???!!!

"I have given the world to the Faithful. There are necessary plans laid out to bring Me back the dirty, the ugly, the nasty and the vulgar. This is not a small task! This is not light work! This is work to fight all evil! The anger and sadness breaks My Heart, for I CREATED WITH JUST A THOUGHT THE WORLD YOU ARE LIVING IN! AND I CREATED WITH JUST A THOUGHT WHAT I WANTED MY PEOPLE TO BE! AND NOW THEY ARE WORSE THAN ROTTEN GARBAGE!

"You asked Me to come again, but I have come in graveness. I have come in sadness, Child; for I will not always come in joy. I AM!!! I AM!!! I AM!!! Revenge is the work of your world. Justice is the Work of My doing! JUSTICE WILL BE DELIVERED, FOR THEY HAVE

TRIED TO DESTROY WHAT I AM CREATING; AND NO ONE WILL DESTROY WHAT I BRING TOGETHER!

+ + +

"'Jesus, have mercy on me!' is the definition of LOVE: MY LOVE of MY SON, SUFFERING FOR YOU! - My Love of My People being saved! It is the Power that many forget! Love Me, and all is well!"

TEACHING on THE IMPORTANCE of BAPTISM

"As a baby, you are born in sin. You become filled with My Spirit when you go through Baptism. Being conscious of My Spirit is a different matter: as you age, you either become more aware of My Presence or you push away. Baptism gives you access to become filled again by My Spirit as you grow closer to Me. If you are not baptized and are growing closer to Me, you do not feel the same intensity and joy of My Spirit!

"Furthermore, if you were not baptized from early on, you could not accept My Spirit from within. The Holy Spirit would be a Shield around you, but *not in you*! That is why Baptism is so crucial! When I got baptized, I did not require it; but in doing so, I was filled with The Spirit, as well as The Spirit emanated from Me!

"The Father, the Son and the Holy Spirit: The Father existed, the Son became flesh, but the Holy Spirit connected the Two together. In doing so, He connected you to Me in a chain that only sin can break."

TEACHING on THE LORD SPEAKS MORE in SILENCE THAN in WORDS

"You may not always hear Me clearly, but it does not mean that I AM not here. I AM always here, but sometimes I speak more in silence than in words! As you embark on a new journey of growth, instead of stagnating, you will face new attacks. But they cannot touch you as you grow stronger in Me! The attacks are meant to make you weak and to fear, but this has not been achieved; for you are stronger now. Where you are, I AM! My Name will save in all situations!

"Remember, if you cannot hear me, it does not mean I AM not there! Rejoice in renewal, growth and praise. I AM always present, even in silence."

TEACHING on: "I TREAT MY CHILDREN with LOVE and TENDERNESS"

"My Child, why are you so frustrated; don't you see how I handle My Children with love and tenderness? You need to be gentler and more tender; for this person is in a lot of trouble, and you cannot be affected by his choices. Let go, move forward, and thank Me always! Tenderness is essential in catering to others, especially in times of tribulation. When you get upset, remember to just say, 'Thank You, Father', and bless them!

"You have learned a lesson that will be lasting; however, it can come at a high price. What happens to another's decision is not on you, but what you are responsible for is not aiding in wrong behaviour! That person will make their own choices; therefore, their own downfalls and uprisings. Do not take that on as your responsibility! You have been a great example."

TEACHING on OBEDIENCE and TRUST

"You do not have to always understand everything; you just need to learn to obey without question. Sometimes the best surprises happen when you do not realize it. Obey Me, and you will be overjoyed. Stop asking questions! Follow the Path I have laid out for you day-by-day. Remember, rest up; you will need it! Trust me and My Path for you.

Follow My Path! You will know when you are falling off it; I will prove it!

"<u>Mark 5: Jesus heals the possessed man</u>. Your story is one of testimony. Your testimony is your experience and path. Whichever path you choose to take, will result in an outcome of your doing! Money is just paper; but faith is ecclesiastical. So, why would you worry about paper? Paper is useless - it will burn! But faith cannot burn; and faith will make you blossom."

<u>TEACHING on LETTING the HURT CHILD GO, and GROWING UP!</u>

"You need to let the hurt child go! You have been through trauma; but you need to let yourself go, and grow up! Let Me hold you up! Trust Me, and I will guide you. There are big changes, therefore:

- Fast;
- Confess;
- Repent;
- Pray;
- Trust Me;
- Love Me.

"What else does your heart seek? Do My Work, HEAR My Voice, follow My Steps, and I shall guide you regarding:

- Weight loss;
- Husband;
- Finances;
- Work;
- Joy!

"Get serious, Child! Get serious! I will speak to you in dreams very often. Get serious, and know it is Me! I AM, and I AM here!"

TEACHING on LOVE YOURSELF; THEN YOU CAN LOVE OTHERS

"Do not love Me and forget yourself! Love Me, but love yourself! It is very important to love yourself. It is very important, because The Father loved you to create you! In order to follow My Commandments and My Will, loving yourself is in wanting the best for yourself: which is Me - My Will, My Blessings and My Salvation!

"I see all your sins. I see all the mistakes, wrong paths and ignorance. But in all the wrong, I see your love, faith and patience to reach Me! That is why sin is overlooked. This does not give a free pass to continue to sin, for then it becomes a routine; and a routine becomes a way-of-living. Slowly it controls, and takes over your sense of righteousness. That is why repentance is so vital, because it allows you to feel righteous again.

"Water pours like honey, but honey does not pour like water until it is warmed. Honey is sweet, and savory, and rich. Pour out your water in sweet, savory richness. In everything you do, do it with love! Do it with a heart for Me! Do it with richness for Me! Water is easy to pour; honey is not! So keep your heart warm, loving and available!

"I will leave you with this! The smell of a rose is sweet. The taste of honey is sweet. The sting of The Father is the sweetest; for He Loves in His Discipline, and He loves in His Mercy! As you taste honey, remind yourself of The Father's Sweetness; and praise Him for all honey!"

TEACHING on GIVING, and HELPING A STRANGER

"The stranger, who asked for help, is a rendition of Me in many ways. Your love to help was rekindled in this experience, for your need to help surpassed your own needs! This is what it means to live in Me: to help, regardless of your own inhibitions!

"This stranger was a key to unlock your selflessness, for that was your main goal when you started your journey. Along the way, it became easy to forget the goal, and focus on selfishness. For when you were weak, alone and in great need, I had My Own People present to help you. Now when others are weak, alone and in need, they will have you to help; for it is easy to say, but hard to do.

"Your example of love is the ultimate key that unlocked the love of a stranger, the love of the unknown, and the faith in My being able to prevail in situations of need! All were revealed with your open heart and open door. As you asked, 'I feel like doing something, but what?' Well, I answered your feelings in this lesson! And it was a lesson not only for you; but for the stranger, and your companion: to see that there are people, MY PEOPLE, who will follow the needs of The Spirit to help, and show exactly what godly love is!

"You have My People to learn from, and you have MY TEACHINGS and Love. But none of these truly matter if your heart is not in the right place. So yes, it is a lesson! Perhaps your friend will learn to love more, without restriction, than to doubt. The enemy will use all situations to his advantage; but when True Love is required, the enemy will have nothing to do with it!

"A broken, shattered, weak and humbled person will forever have gratitude to a stranger, rather than a person who is proud and stands tall! As you said, now you have a stranger praying for you; and that is the ultimate blessing in that situation!"

TEACHING on DREAMS

"Dreams are a form of reality! When you cannot control your reality, how do you expect to live off your choices? Reality is your subconscious. It is where the enemy will attack the most. Often I will speak in dreams, because you surrender your conscious, and do not fight! At the same time, the same rule applies to the enemy.

"Was I speaking in your dream? Why were you afraid? Is it because you saw the face of the enemy? Have faith and hope! All is possible! When you let go, you give Me room to reach out more! When you stop caring for your position, you allow yourself further growth. When you release, you have more room to fill. The same with the demons: when you release them, you have more room to fill with My Love!"

TEACHING on CELEBRATING THE LORD'S LOVE on ST. VALENTINE'S DAY

"How many celebrated My Love with them today? Even in solidarity, it is My Love celebrated! Celebrate My Love first, then yours: My Union first! You do this when you get married! You celebrate with Me, then go and celebrate with family and friends! Church is My Union; the reception is yours. Valentine's is My Celebration of Love with you, then yours replicated!"

TEACHING on CELEBRATING FATHER'S DAY

"Have you celebrated your 'Father's Day'? Have you honoured 'The Father' for all that He has done, and continues to do? Have you given Him thanks and blessings? You may have sent out a message to all your friends to love, honour, and be grateful for their fathers; but did you say the same to 'The Father'? The Father is the only 'Father' out there who deserves all honour, praise and thanksgiving! Do not forget to honour Him! Remember, all is because HE IS!"

TEACHING on THE FATHER'S LOVE

"'The love which a father has for His child is not comparable until the child has one of his own?' What then is to be said to people who do not have children; that they cannot understand the love of a father? To love is to turn around, to mute your ears, to bring a cup of water and make a meal!

"'To love is to hate, is to hit, is to yell, is to punish?' But what is the source of that 'love'? How easy it is to classify everything under 'love'; but is it godly Love or worldly 'love'?

"The love of a child to its Father is growing, everlasting, nurturing and gratifying! The love of a child is unique and mighty: for it shares the cries, the joys, the pain, the gain, the health and the wealth! It shares in passion, in grief, in laughter and sorrow! It shares collectively, and abundantly! Share My Love, speak of My Love and teach My Love!"

TEACHING on PATIENCE

"Child, Child, you must learn patience! You do not command Me to speak, and I speak! It is only when I choose to speak, that I speak! In My Grace, I AM always around; but Child, patience until I choose to respond!

"Patience is very important for what I have planned for you. Patience has been applied in all areas of your life; for everything, you have waited a very long time, and you are still waiting! I taught in patience, I taught slowly, and I taught with deliberate intention. When I did not have to speak, I did not. Be still, My Child! Learn to be still. Impatience is lucifer's specialty; with it comes mistakes, eagerness, miscalculations and errors in judgment. Think back to all the mistakes done in your past; were they done in patience or impatience?

"What I AM teaching you is Wisdom; but you should not feel that others cannot teach you as well. For I speak through many people, even though I speak directly to you. It is a learning process. I, too, must be patient to wait for My People to return to Me. I, too, must be patient to wait for you to give Me your attention!"

TEACHING on SHOWERING with LOVE, KINDNESS and PEACE

"Stop complaining about the weather, Child! The more you complain, the less you will appreciate the beauty that comes from rain. If it was hot and humid, you would also complain. When it is cold and snowy, you complain as well. Try complaining about something that you can accomplish in changing, not the weather! However, to complain is a bad trait; for it shows how selfish and ungrateful you can be!

"Complaining is the work of the enemy. Try walking outside and saying, 'Thank You Lord, for Your Rain has created organic fruits that nothing can compare to in taste. Thank You Lord, for the rain has washed the grass from all the pesticides, and helps the animals live and flourish'. How about, 'Thank You Lord, for it is Your Will to rain today'? You have to work on this, to reach a level of understanding and maturity to not complain about situations. Until that level has been accomplished, you will not see all My efforts in changing and helping you.

"Child, you were typing and saying how the sun was bothering your sight. You were saying how it was creating a glare. But when I provide a solution, why do you take it so harshly? Where is the love and kindness I AM teaching you? You cannot take a simple act and praise Me, and say thank You? Instead you are ready to complain.

"I can teach you, but it is My style of teaching that you need to learn to be helpful to others. I could have come out and said, 'Stop complaining, Child!', and 'Stop being so selfish'! However, I came with Humour, and Kindness and Love. You were ready to listen, because I showed Love above all else. Try showing more love to people before you speak to them! You can shower them with love, kindness and peace to create a change in them!"

TEACHING on GIVING THE LORD the GLORY

"When you are asked about MY Gifts and Blessings, be sure to say, 'It is The Lord!' and not, 'Thanks to God'; for it is I WHO fulfilled MY Promise to you! Thanking Me is beautiful, but that leaves room for assumptions you are doing it yourself. It is ONLY I Who made these Gifts and Blessings possible!"

TEACHING on REMAINING TRUE to YOUR HEART

"Why worry about something so insignificant? Will I not take care of you? Remain true to your heart, and nothing contrary shall prevail."

CHAPTER 4

WHY SEEK ME?

TEACHING on COMPOSITION OF PRAYER

"Some people do not know how to pray. There is no right way to pray, but there are three steps, like writing an essay: There is a thesis, a middle section of points, and a conclusion. The thesis is inviting Me into the prayer: it is making the request. The essence of the prayer has to revolve around gratitude, love and willingness to surrender. The reason why two people together reunite My Presence in prayer is because their spiritual braids join together and form a Trinity - I AM the Third Part of that Trinity.

"Let us pray:

> *'My Father in Heaven, where all royalty begins and ends; where all existence begins and ends; where the Light is shining, and the darkness is but an old dream; where evil longs to see but cannot, and breathe but cannot. Father in Heaven, Glory be to You The Almighty! Glory be to You, for you know Love like no other; and You cherish every tear dropped and every hair grown.*

'May Your Servants be as dedicated to You as Your Angels are, and may they love You as they love their desires. May they realize Your Guidance and Your Direction, for You are the Only One Who will pave the Path to safety! May Your Feathers be mighty and strong, and carry them through the fiercest winds; and may they grip onto You now and eternally. May You bless them with each blink of an eye, and kiss them with each breath taken; for Your Lips are Purity, and Your Blessings are Golden, which no fire can melt, and no evil can taint.

'May Your Chosen be as virtuous and righteous as I was; but may they realize their sufferings will be Mine to endure, and rejoice in that comfort! Power to The Father to give, for all His Children are His Mark! May You be pleased with them, and forgive them in all their misgivings; for there is no other father worthy of praise, other than You! Amen.

<u>TEACHING on: "TIME SPENT with ME!"</u>

"Time is non-existent in My World, but in yours it is as fierce as death! It can come in an instant, and leave you in shambles; or it can bring you the greatest joy! Time is a figment of reality that is altered and used by the enemy: to diminish faith and strength, to cause doubt and weaken confidence, and to frustrate and make late. Time is essential; at least it is essential in your minds. Remove the concept of time, and you will feel freedom. Time is the essence to nothing, for there is no time in My Realm; yet time is essential for your daily lives. Be sure to incorporate My Definition of time with yours, and combine both to live in harmony.

"It is easy for Me to fast-track your life. If I was to move ahead, how would you experience your joys and sorrows? How would you realize what effects your decisions make? Yes, I can take you up tonight, but then what? How would you move forward in character development, and help others here on earth? It is how you use every moment, and how you move forward in each moment!

"Never, in a moment, regret what you are feeling, change your feelings, wish to be somewhere else, or wish to feel something else! For you choose everything that you feel, and the circumstances you experience. The moments and circumstances will alter your life at times, bringing you such joys and sorrow. At the end of the journey, if your eyes are on Me, it will bring you back to Me! Never, in a moment, forget My Love or My Touch! I AM here in this moment, with your sorrow and joy!

"You need to realize it takes more than being a Christian and praying to follow Me! Time dissipates when you are not strong in faith. You need to spend more time in My Word, My Writings, My Teachings - in My Faith! You need to spend more time learning what My Teachings mean to your decisions! Time with Me is time gained and reproduced! Time with Me is rejuvenation - a Blessing and a Gift! Why do you not spend time with Me? Why do you not spend thirty minutes with Me? Why do you not spend time with Me?

"I can only be there to help if I AM welcomed! How can I help and lead if you do not allow My Presence into your life? I AM here and you are there; but I cannot be with you unless you open the door of your heart, and let Me enter! You need to spend more time in allowing Me to answer! It is not just speaking to Me; it is giving Me the chance to reply!"

TEACHING on TIME MANAGEMENT

"There is always time for Me! There is always time for My Presence to shine! Your choices will take you by; time is nothing but an illusion. Time with Me is 'Time-in-existence' - from there, to here, to Eternity!

"Time management is not a concern for you, but choosing the right time in your time is your concern! Learn to decipher what is important to you. You already know what is right and wrong, but your ability to answer is based on your weakness. Stand up and realize that I have your back! So do not worry, and manage your time in peace.

"It is easy to state the obvious; it is easy to say 'yes'; and it is easy to put things on hold for later - but later may not come. Wouldn't you rather do what is right to be done on time, than to keep it for later, and not have that moment come? So answer these questions:

- Am I listening to The Lord speak through His Word, and giving Him the thanksgiving and praise that is due His Name?
- If time was to end tomorrow, would I be satisfied with how I spent my last moments?
- Am I in peace?

"Do more for your soul than for others. Spend more time to help your soul revive, than what you do for others. You have the time now to spend alone. There will be a time when you will have wished you had more time for yourself, and quality time is needed to improve and accomplish your desires.

"All will be clear as you spend more time with Me; which includes workouts, reading, and cleaning - any alone-time is time with Me! The more you spend time with Me, the more your heart will grow with Mine, and learn to Love as Mine.

"The enemy enjoys being in control. When he sees Me, he loses control and creates chaos! Chaos is fear, and chaos is power. Why would I give the enemy extra power, especially if he knows who I AM? WHO I AM! I AM ALL-EMPOWERING! I AM POWER, but I AM All-Empowering!"

TEACHING on PROTECTING YOUR HEART

"What is it that you are seeking? What is it that you are wanting? What has changed in the past short days to have you uneasy and unsettled? Do you have answers to these questions? Do you realize that you are under attack to fall? It is time to strengthen the walls, and to clay the cracks. Be sure to be on The Lord's Side to receive the Blessings; otherwise, the enemy will create disasters out of the opportunities.

"How do you strengthen the shaky walls? Child, when you are in My Battle, the attacks will NEVER stop! It is as timeless as your faith in Me! As long as you have faith, you have reason to be attacked! You have to keep your walls nailed together. Remember to unite with My Presence, in My Blessings, in My Word, which is the only TRUE WORD!"

TEACHING on MONEY

"This world runs on 'money', and believes money is the answer to all problems! Money is the root of all evil, creating desire, lust, greed and anger. It is the exact opposite of what love creates. The more money you seek and desire, the less you seek Me. Money allows you to forget what it is to be needy - in need of Me!

"Do you not see how easy it would be for Me to bless you in completion financially? If all your problems are resolved instantly, you will not understand how The Father works, and what He desires from you! Money is just a piece of paper: it is nothing of value, nothing that will aid in your stroll through the Gates!

"Do you realize that suffering financially is a figment of your imagination, and is mundane? However, if you are stable in My Presence, then you will not have to water the 'seed' of provision; for it would flourish in its own time - with your blessing."

TEACHING on: "THE LORD SPEAKS THE LANGUAGE OF MUSIC"

"If I reveal Myself to you in My Presence, you will be too afraid, and will turn away. But as I reveal Myself to you in familiar ways, you are willing. My sight is very frightening for you; but Child, I AM nothing but peaceful! There will come a time when I can reveal Myself to you, and know that you will not turn away. Do not fear! Did I frighten you, or did I leave you in peace?

"Continue calling on Me, seeking Me, covering yourself in My Presence! When you sleep, I will come and see you; but you must have faith in this, Child. You questioned My Presence in front of you; however, your subconscious is your conscious state in the spirit world! You are free in your subconscious; and therefore, it is your true reality!

"Why do you fear seeing demonic entities? Don't you see you have the power to cast them aside? THEY are afraid of you! Do not be afraid, Child; for they cannot harm you or hurt you. They are just trying to enter. Remember, they are always around.

"You asked if it was My Will for you to go on vacation; and I waited a whole week for you to declare, 'I do not want to go if it is not Your Will'! Then I could give you My Blessings! *Don't you see, it is the awareness of doing My Will before yours that gives Me the ability to bless you.*

"Child, you need to continue to seek Me, to live in Me, and to pray to Me in your time of need. What did I say the last time? Speak My Name, and I will be there to fight alongside you. Speak My Name, and

I will battle for you! All you have to remember is to speak My Name! If all My Children would remember to speak My Name in their time of struggle, then the enemy would have no warriors with which to battle! My Name has lived on and on, and My Name carries the world! Speak My Name, and I shall be there. This I promise you!

"Let us pray tonight. I will pray tonight:

> *'Encompassing Father, Loyal Warrior, Graceful and Majestic King, Mighty and Powerful Lord: with You we are honored and loved, with You we are healed and alive. You fight our battles! You fight our temptations with Your Scepter, pointed and ready to battle and defend. Your Breath is Divine, and Pure and Holy; Your Love is unimaginable! Your Army of Angels is ready to protect and battle! With time ticking by Your Side, We are given another breath to breathe, another opportunity to repent, and another moment to love! Bless us, Oh Royal King! Bless us, Oh Humble and Devout King! For no one is greater than You, and no one is Holier than You! Shine Your Light on these people, and shower them with Your Peace! Show them Your Divine World, and let them shine for everyone to see!*
>
> *'Bless You, Oh Lord, Oh Majesty, Oh King! Bless You and thank You; for Your loving Heart forgives all, and grants them eternal Peace! Please cover them tonight, and allow them to grow in Your Spirit. Love them with Your Grace, and protect them from evil. Teach them, and let them shine for You! I pray in Your Name, Oh Father, Oh King, Oh beloved Majesty. I pray to You, Oh High One, for Your Love has blessed these people for eternity. May they live to make You glorified!'*

"For now, the night is calling you. Sleep, pray and love until the light shines again. Amen."

TEACHING on "ONE-ON-ONE - THE FULL CYCLE OF LOVE"

"'One-on-one' can be with two people, or it can be with yourself, alone. What does 'one-on-one' mean to you? It is beautiful to share My Word with others - a Gift in itself! But always remember to have 'One-on-One' with Me before you have your 'one-on-one' with others. I believe your 'one-on-one' is more meaningful after My 'One-on-One'! It is a blessed experience to see another improve in the journey of life.

"Let us pray:

- *1, 2, 3: Your love is with Me; now let's carry that 4, 5, 6: You rise up in Me; 7, 8, 9: You surrender to Me; 10, 11, 12: You reach for Me; 13, 14, 15: Let's do it again!*
- *1, 2, 3: My Love is with you; 4, 5, 6: I rose for you; 7, 8, 9: I carried your sins; 10, 11, 12: I cleaned your stains; 13, 14, 15: Let's do it again!*
- *1, 2, 3: Love is between; 4, 5, 6: Love is carried; 7, 8, 9: Love is clean; 10, 11, 12: Love is revealed; 13, 14, 15: Love is enduring - 'The Full Cycle of Love'.*"

TEACHING on RAYS OF THE SUN:

- A day that begins with rays of the sun is a day to celebrate the beauty of My Creation;
- A day that begins with the Light of My Light, is a day to rejoice in My Existence;
- A day that begins with My Existence is a day of Salvation.

"My Work is finally coming together. When The Father plans, it is only His Will that will preside! The people and events do not matter, as long as His Will is fulfilled; but He chooses for their good, their honour and their Salvation. The choices made are their own to follow through.

"Follow the rays of The Son, follow the Rays of My Light, and follow My Existence; for they will lead you to Blessings and Glory."

TEACHING on PASCHAL PRAYER FOR THE DECEASED

"On the 8th night of Paschal, we thank the Spirits for watching over us. We bless them, for one day we will join them; and we recognize their efforts.

"Let us pray:

'In Our Father, all is given; in Our Father, all is taken. We thank You for what You have given, and We thank You for what You have taken. We bless them in Your Honour and Name, and We thank You. Amen.'

CHAPTER 5

TEMPTATIONS, TRIALS and TRIBULATIONS

TEACHING on "YOU MUST CHOOSE ME FIRST!"

"Child, choose Me! Choose Me! Choose Me, and I will deliver all you seek! Choosing Me entails trusting Me, and allowing Me to rule! What may seem great may not always be the case later on. Child, this is natural, this is normal; but it is intensified and magnified, for you are going through momentous trials in a short period of time. I cannot help you if you do not turn to Me! In this time, you are growing and maturing at such a speed, you cannot comprehend all the changes, or what is happening. Remember, I go through everything with you. Don't you see that I AM a forgiving and loving Lord?

"You must choose Me first! All these temptations and trials will make you stronger, and will make you unbreakable and untouchable; but you have to go through these first to reach that point. Believe Me, this is a temptation for the good, not the bad. There are good temptations, and there are bad temptations. This is for the good. I AM teaching you, and I AM testing you to choose Me in every single moment of your reality! As I said, there will be more to come, but you must pass this obstacle first! You did not like that last statement, clearly, as you stopped listening. Oh Child, this is how you will grow; for you grow in experience, and not in warning!

"Open The Word - <u>Isaiah 12</u>: This is what you say to people when they ask about you, your progress, and your belief. Study this passage often, for it is a direct reminder of how I have blessed you, and continue to bless you. The clock is ticking! You have a short period left to receive all the anointed blessings; but you have a short period of temptation. TIME IS ALMOST UP, CHILD! TIME IS ALMOST OVER, CHILD! TIME IS ALMOST UP, CHILD! IT IS ALMOST OVER. WILL YOU ACTUALLY BE BLESSED, OR WILL YOU FAIL? THE ANSWER IS YET TO BE SEEN; BUT I AM GIVING YOU A STREAM TO DRINK FROM, AND A PASSAGE TO SHINE AND PASS THROUGH ALL TRIALS AND TEMPTATIONS! CHOOSE ME, AND YOU WILL BE HONORED, AND YOU WILL BE SAVED, AND YOU WILL BE MINE!

"<u>Ezekiel 33</u> - This is the Path of your journey, Child. This is the Path of your journey! This is what you have been chosen for: to speak My Words, and to warn and change lives. And if they hear you, they will be saved and seek My Salvation. If they do not hear you, then they will burn; for it is My Word they are turning away from. They will all know one day that you were sent from Me, whether it is the time of their acceptance, or the time of their demise; but they will all be aware when they will not be able to say, 'I did not know', 'I was not warned', or 'I did not have an opportunity!'

"Obeying Me does not always give you the key to receive what you want. Obeying Me gives you the ability to receive My Blessing, but it is not a guarantee. The Father knows best, and He decides what is best for you."

TEACHING on WORDS OF WISDOM

"Child, why are you doing this? Why do you watch other people's celebrations, only to feel sad about yours? Do you not see that this is the work of the enemy: how he infiltrated your mind to feel sorrow watching these videos of weddings and celebration? You already know what is to come for you! Why must you get sad? You have the greatest Gift of all: My personal contact with you! Child, do not let your mind lose focus on Me; because when it does, this is what happens: the enemy puts a foot into the door!

"Please be more careful! I AM here, and I AM with you! I have made a Covenant with you to give you your heart's desires, one by one, as long as I AM in your forefront! That is the only way you will follow the right Path to Me, and your desires will be fulfilled along that Path! Child, listen to My Words very carefully:

> 'There once was a girl, a very lonely girl;
> There once was a girl, a very lonely girl.
> There once was a boy, a very lonely boy;
> There once was a boy, a very lonely boy.
>
> 'There once was a girl, who turned her life to Christ;
> There once was a girl, who turned her life to Christ.
> There once was a boy, who prayed for a Holy Life;
> There once was a boy, who prayed for a Holy Life.
>
> 'There once was a girl, who finally found her knight;
> There once was a girl, who finally found her knight.
> There once was a boy, who finally found his wife;
> There once was a boy, who finally found his wife.'

"A wise man once said, 'To be humble is one of the greatest blessings of all; better to be humble now than to fall later.' It is easy to walk, but difficult to stand tall. Do not be afraid to stand tall, but learn how to walk while standing tall. Often you may stumble; but if your core is stable, you will rise up again. It is easy to get your head in the clouds. Sometimes I have to pull you down, but this applies to many. Do not be afraid to speak up, but be cautious; for when you speak, your words release consequences. But do not worry, for your actions will produce different results."

TEACHING on "SPREAD YOUR WINGS, and FLY OVER the FOG!"

"When I say seek Me, you must seek! Look at all these people living in confusion. They cannot see ahead. The white fog is a cloud, confusing with misjudgment, chaos and misunderstanding. Can you see across to the other side - down, to the other side? Look up, what do you see? Do not let yourself be carried away, for you will not see through the cloud. Spread your wings, and soar like an eagle: go fly! Do you see through the clouds? You do not want to fall. You can make it across, and you can see. This is how you have seen the last few days, through milk or a cloud.

"Come! What do you see? Listen, you can hear music! But the music is changing to screaming voices, and the water to blood - too much blood-shed! This is why you must stay on track! This is what I hear; but I cannot help them or touch them, because they do not believe. But you can help them, for you believe! You do not want this blood on your hands! As easy as it turns to blood, you can keep it as a waterfall! Spread your wings, and fly under the waterfall! See the cities below you. After all this, there is only this many praying! See how few have faith! Choose Me, and believe! Come! Come!

"See the joy of life - but it is not joy! It is all black and red! It is like an underground city! Why don't you take a swim? Why don't you go and explore? This is where you are all living! How many times do you fall? There will come a time when I will not pick you up!"

TEACHING on CLEANSING

> *"'Do you always need warning signs to believe it is I coming? Do you always need to feel the recurring signs to know I AM here? In My Home, I speak. This is My Home, do not worry.*
>
> *"I can bring you pain and discomfort, but I Love you too much to bring you pain. I have waited a long time! I continue to wait, for I AM Patient; but My Patience has limits! I create, I do not destroy; but I can bring down destruction! I AM Patient, but it has limits! I create as easily as I destroy. Without My Blessing, nothing is left! Pray to receive blessings! Through prayer, all is delivered!*
>
> *"Do you doubt My Presence now, Child? My Gift of Communication is a Gift of Honour! Realize this, and praise Me, Child!'"*

"I AM always here, Child! I AM always here, but The Father made His Presence known! You need more deliverance, Child; but now is not the time. Slowly, you will go through it. This is a period of filtering and rejuvenation. Spend time in The Word, rest, eat, sleep, pray - and know that it is a time to filter out all the weeds, sift through the fertilizer, and get ready to grow and blossom!"

TEACHING on FAITH IS KEY!

"As long as you are open, I can use you greatly as a messenger. But you need to work on your issues with faith:

- Continue moving forward;
- Be careful whom you speak to regarding this topic of faith;

THE LAST MESSAGE

- It is a journey to follow Me; but one that requires a lot of faith - a lot of blind faith!

"<u>Open The Word - Joshua 22: Witnesses</u>. That is the key! To have witnesses around means you are not creating such things in your head! To have faith is to stand and say, 'I believe blindly'! It is a Gift, but to doubt is a curse! Remember to be grateful! Remember to thank Me, and remember to love Me - for I have loved you, and blessed you, and trusted you. But I cannot do it all on My own. I need your cooperation. Trust Me! You are not wise enough, you are not all-knowing, and you are selfish as a being. You do not have the ability of The Father and of His Love and Mercy to pass on as your own! You are just human; but you are a channel and funnel used to share My Messages, and direct others to My Thoughts.

"I will help you, and introduce you to others who have similar Gifts; and you will see that all you have learned and experienced are common to My chosen People. Others sense the Holy Spirit, and feel as you do when I arrive. This is just one example of commonalities. To believe means you give others an opportunity to believe in Me, as well.

"By year end, you will have your own support; but to receive this, you must be 100% faithful, and loving Me! How many years have you prayed for My choice of husband? Well now that I AM ready, you are not! You see, faith and the enemy cannot work together: trust, fight, faith and mercy!

> *"Father, have mercy on these people, and bless them! Have mercy, and bless them, for they are just humans."*

<u>TEACHING on LISTENING CAREFULLY!</u>

> *"I AM a God of Love, Forgiveness, Patience and Comfort; but I cannot be that type of God if you do*

not give Me blind faith! You require help? You must make the first move, and ask for it; then wait for it to be given. You require My Help, but I cannot help you if you cannot believe in My Greatness! Understand, all My People, it is always so easy to ask for something; but if you do not believe it or seek it willingly, I cannot grant it or help or flourish it! I AM not a God Who listens and does! I AM a God Who needs unconditional faith and love to help in all situations. Without that faith, I cannot help!

"I have proven Myself over and over again! Why must I be shafted? Why must I be pushed aside, and only needed when there is great suffering or desire? I AM so very sad! My People forget so easily all that I have done for them! REMIND them! REMIND YOURSELF!

"I AM very sad, My Child! I AM very, very sad, My Child! My Heart is heavy, and full of sorrow and grief. Why is it so difficult to follow instructions? Why is it so difficult to listen, especially if it is for the best? Why are there so many conflicts and oppositions regarding My Instructions? My People! Why can they not follow instructions, especially if it is for their best?

"Does a life have to be lost for them to humble themselves and follow Me? Does something so drastic and severe have to happen for My People to listen and humble themselves? My Greatness is as strong as your faith in Me! My Power is as mighty as your faith in Me! I cannot help you if you cannot turn to Me!

"My Cycle begins with unconditional blind faith, and ends with unconditional blind faith! WHERE IS MY FAITH? Where has the faith disappeared to? TWO THOUSAND YEARS AGO, FAITH WAS BLIND; AND NOW IT IS STILL BLIND! When will you people wake up? I AM a God Who wants the best for you, and Who wants to make everything great! But why must you complicate and dirty the water by not listening? Listen!!! LISTEN TO MY VOICE!!! LISTEN TO MY VOICE! For if I go mute, your days are numbered, and your time is up!!!

"I AM addressing My People! LISTEN!!! I said this before, MY PEOPLE!!! Why do they not understand that the only way I can help is if I have the door of your heart open to walk through? I AM so sad! I AM so very disappointed! I cannot speak of My Sorrow! My grief-filled Sorrow drowns me! I AM so very sad! It is time to harvest, and it is time to sow; it is time to fertilize, and it is time to grow!"

TEACHING on FOCUS

"I have been waiting to speak to you. When you give me your undivided attention, I AM ready to speak!

"Today's theme is 'Focus': where do you focus your attention? What you put your focus on becomes your reality! Yesterday, you were caught up by the enemy, because your focus was on something other than Me. That is not to say you were sinning, but you got absorbed in your desires. You were having difficulty focusing on Me from the conversations around you, to your voice-messages. I know it is difficult, but you must try harder! As you can see now, you are able to type clearly without having to re-edit, because you are actually listening to My Voice!

"You must realize the importance of starting the day with Me! You will be speaking My Words, and not what you believe to be correct! If I had not warned you last night about temptation today, and making many choices, would you be as confident right now as you are? My People always have a way out; but can they always hear Me speaking to them? It is up to them to hear My Voice, and act on it!

"Remember, 'Focus' is the theme today. All your choices are based on focus. As you can see, you have many choices to make today; are you making the right ones?

"Choices: The first part of your day has come and passed. Have you made the right choices? Did My Disciples make the right choices after I left them? How did they know they were on the Path to Righteousness? You may not always understand My Nudges, My soft Whispers, or My Direction; but when the time passes, My Plan is revealed to you!

"Do you realize how hard it is to focus on Me today? Do you see how much you are struggling to hear My Voice? You need to FOCUS! Just sit still in My Presence, and focus on Me! I AM here. I AM always here! Let My Love guide you, and steer you clear of all temptations. You have been good. I will encourage you, and give you strength; but there is a lot of work to be done. And it will take very strict focus, as you will understand later on."

<u>TEACHING on "THE BRIDGE" - HOW TO FLEE TEMPTATION, and HOW TO STAY FOCUSED on THE LORD</u>

"Walking on a bridge is much like the journey you are on with Me. You awake with days of immense beauty on all corners: from the lavish pastures, to the bright sky above, to the colours flowing around, revealing the artwork of The Father. Then you have days where all you see around you is dry, empty, cold land; and dark, heavy and polluted air. As I stated, walking on a bridge is much like the journey you are on. Some days you walk straight and forward; other days you stumble on different stones, and can trip and fall or redirect your path. Depending on the route, you will experience different terrain and different visibility. It is easy to get lost in such circumstances; for when you cannot see forward, you cannot be sure you are moving ahead and not backwards.

"How to flee temptation, how to steer forward, staying focused on Me: many of the difficulties endured and struggles have been because of disobedience; however, it was also judgment for tripping and falling off the Path on which you were guided by Me alone!

"I AM going to teach you how to flee temptation, and how to stay focused on Me:

- You wake up praising The Father. To praise The Father is to pray to Him, to honor Him, and to worship His Majesty and Love;
- You open up The Word to hear His Direction, Warning or Love. This is to be done even before you start your day;
- You mark yourself against the enemy: arm yourself with My Cross; for when the enemy sees The Cross, he knows his time is limited, and he will be crushed beneath the weight of your faith! When the enemy sees The Cross, he sees defeat! Instead of wearing it, you can always carry The Cross with you. It is a reminder for you and the enemy, not for showing;
- You start your daily journey in prayer. You compare all your actions to your faith, to The Cross! When you become tempted, and the enemy is shining in front of you, you focus on The Cross, and how that frees you from the enemy. You focus on My Strength to save you, My Love to free you, and the enemy's defeat at My Feet!
- When you focus on Me, the enemy does not have a chance to misguide you, confuse you, or tempt you; for your attention is on Me alone! When you have moments when you forget to

focus on Me, the enemy has the ability to enter. This is often the situation with you - the enemy enters when you forget Me! But again, My Cross will help you to fight! When you realize you are in temptation, pray to Me, and seek My Help! Surrender yourself to Me, and allow Me to take over, to fight the enemy with My Spirit;

- To praise Me is to accept My Presence in your life;
- When you cannot see, hear or understand, then seek Me in unity! Seek Me in unity, and again you shall find a route back to Me;
- In falling for temptation, you may feel joy, peace, love, desire and want fulfilled; but it will only last a few moments, before you are filled with guilt, hurt, anger and negativity;
- Return home on your knees! Return home facing Me, regardless of all sins, temptations and failures. Return home to Me repentant, humbled and realizing you cannot walk on this journey without stumbling - even when you try your best to focus on Me alone. Thank and praise Me, for I AM here with you holding your hand, whispering in your ear, and soothing your aching heart. Thank Me and praise Me for keeping your legs steady, so when you stumble and fall, and redirect your path, I AM here to guide you back and set you free! Thank and praise Me, for I AM here! Even when you forget to speak to Me, ignore My Words, and pretend all is well (for you were fooled by the enemy, and believe you are still on track), thank and praise Me! I AM here to wash the stains of your foolish acts so that you may return to The Father in love, joy and thanksgiving, knowing that nothing is as wonderful, loving, patient and peaceful as this experience in relationship with Me!

"You had many dreams. You are afraid to see what you ask to be revealed to you, yet you continue to ask to have things revealed. How can I reveal things to you without frightening you? Yes, what you have seen is true.

What you see allows you to understand how ugly the real nature of the enemy is! This is a blessing for you to see!

"When you fail, or are tempted, or filled with the enemy, your spirit too is filled, and covered, and struggling to breathe! You can use this to explain, in the future, what it is to be filled with the enemy, to require deliverance, and truly how ugly the enemy really is! When you ask for things to be revealed, be sure to ask for the grace to accept it without fear; and to have total understanding that The Lord is with you in all consciousness.

"My Child, I AM proud of how you are handling your trials. You are more conscious of evil around you. Work even harder! We are going to move quickly. You are going to blossom very quickly with an outpour of Wisdom and Knowledge.

✝ ✝ ✝

"My Child, I have a very stern warning for you! Do not be fooled by men. I don't want you to be misled by them. The choice is yours, but I'm giving you a stern warning: the enemy is using them to get to you.

"You are going to come across a man, an older man. He is going to need your help. It is up to you: if you have ME in your forefront, you will see him and help him.

✝ ✝ ✝

"I know you are worried about finances; but I promise you, My People and I will take care of you. Then one day, you will take care of others the same way you are being taken care of; you will have your opportunity to tremendously help others financially.

✝ ✝ ✝

"You are teetering back and forth: one foot in, and one foot out. That is the enemy inside you. You must get serious, and renounce all the enemies inside. Cast them out! You know how to do it; you have the Gift! I will be there to help you; but you must renounce them, for they make you weak. Changes are happening, great changes and improvements. But one foot off creates imbalance, and prolongs the journey. Once and for all, cast the demons out so you may stand stable, firm, confident and, most importantly, at peace! Take a decision and act on it, but do not teeter-totter!

"Reading the Bible will help you, as well. You must spend at least one hour in My Word daily! Understand? It is important to do it on your own, so you may build a solid relationship with Me first, then with others; for reading The Word will build your relationships. My Message is strong in unity! The more united you are, the stronger your faith will be. The stronger you will be, for in unity there is more to battle with, especially if I AM your Leader!"

TEACHING on POSITIVITY

"Why is it so difficult to choose Me, to choose My Ways? Why is it always difficult to do the right thing? Have you wondered about these things? Why is it hard to do 'good'? What is the importance of choosing to do 'good'? What is the significance of following My Will?

"<u>Lessons</u>: Life lessons are difficult; but they form character, and they develop maturity. My World is Perfect, My World is Holy, and My World is Light. Your world is sinful, dirty and heavy. You cannot enter My World with your dirt; but you can walk off the dirt, and clean yourself up.

"Without trials, temptations, troubles and triumphs, you will not be able to appreciate My Light, My Glory and My Blessings. When you see hardship, you feel unarmed; but I see decisions! When you feel weak and broken, I see Compassion and Salvation! You cannot do anything without being broken! You cannot pass through this channel of existence without going through trials and struggles; for this process builds, unites, and strengthens what I see to build, and see in you. Remember, there is no time in My World. What you understand now, you may not understand tomorrow.

"To build you, I needed millions of pieces of sand. Do you think they were all perfect? Do you think they were all clean? Do you think they were all arranged to fit together? However, through the imperfections, I created perfection. Do not try to be perfect, for no one is perfect! You cannot be perfect, for you are not your own creator. But you can try to create perfection in your imperfection; you can try to be Holy in your sinful nature; you can try to love in a hateful world! However, do not try to be perfect; for you will fail! If I wanted you to be perfect, I would not have given you free will; for then I would choose all your decisions, thus making you perfect in all you do! You, as a being, are not perfect. My Spirit is Perfect! You share My Spirit!

"Have you fully decided to be with Me, for things will get worse! Can you take the struggle, or will you give up? This is not a challenge or a test, but it is a rite-of-passage: to experience struggle, and to conquer it for the right reasons. Similarly, you are on a journey to discover, to learn, to strengthen, and to grow. That is why you will experience similar paths with others. However, each role is individual, and collectively produces a whole.

"It is time for you to wake up, and move forward: one way or another, to move forward. You are stronger than you think. You are able and willing, but you are surrounded by quick sand! Don't you see that what you feel, and what you are using, are temporary fillers? Don't you see and understand that you are hiding your abilities? You are not fighting! You can conquer all your trials and temptations, but you need to realize your strength that lives in you. You have tremendous strength to achieve greatness, but you choose to weaken yourself!

"Yes, you were weak; but I made you strong! And you were small and broken; but I mended you whole! I mended you Myself, remember? I mended you MYSELF, REMEMBER!!! Do not sit there and feel your weakness, for you insult My Craftsmanship. Do not feel weak, for you are much stronger than you realize. Wake up! Wake up! Wake up! You have to fight! Stop giving in to weakness and temptation, and stand up! If I AM with you - and I AM in you - why would you feel so weak?

"Do you have to relive those moments again to realize what strength you possess? Do you remember your commitment? Well, Child, it is fight time! Why have you given up so easily, and succumbed to feeling so weak and small? Do not let anyone make you feel small or weak; for I, Myself, have made you strong and complete!

"I cannot give you your desires until you realize your potential, for you will waste My Blessings. YOU ARE MIGHTY! When demonic entities see you, they will run; but if you do not feel your strength, how can you stand up against them? You need deliverance, but this deliverance will be done by yourself!"

TEACHING on DISOBEDIENCE and REPENTANCE

"You keep going in circles about the fact that you disobeyed, and only if you had listened to Me months ago . . . ! The reality is that I told you months ago. Everyone has freedom of choice, and the choices they make have consequences. You did not fully understand that concept, because you said, 'Why would anyone not follow "The Words of God?"' Why didn't you? It is not simple. It takes complete and utter blind faith to follow My Words! But as humans, your mentality takes over, and you believe you know best. What you see and touch is your reality, and not what you believe! That is why so many fail.

"Why are you not celebrating? Why are you not happy? Why are you upset and hurting, and why are you doubting? Why are you being weak?

Don't you see the blessings I have brought upon you? Don't you realize the blessings I have brought upon you? Feel hurt now. Cry, and get sad; but remember, this will last seconds compared to a lifetime!

"Unfortunately, My People are narrow-minded. They cannot think past the situation at hand. It is one of the downfalls of humanity, because they cannot understand and foresee what We see! You feel hurt, you feel upset. I AM here to carry you up, and make you rise up above this; but you must give Me the opportunity to do so. During the night, pray and read the Bible.

"Emotional swings are attacks from the enemy, because of your disobedience. There are always repercussions to disobeying My Commands, and they may not always come up instantly. They may take time to filter out. When the attacks are strong, they will cause pain; but you have to fight, and turn to Me when it happens. Do not falter your attention away from Me, and focus on the pain and grief!

"I AM a loving God, a faithful God, a loyal God and a forgiving God; but I have limits to what I can endure, forgive and teach. Each of you has the same option and choice. I cannot always be there to guide you. You have to put in the effort to guide your life to My Path; I will lead the Way. Remember, the more you delay, the longer it will take to reunite with My Path! Do not delay, and follow Me!

"You have to move forward, and move with Me! I will say this again: do not focus on your past mistakes! Just turn to Me. I AM here, I AM your Conversation, I AM your Friendship, I AM your Lover, and I AM your soul-Protector. I AM, Child! I AM. Do not turn away from Me, but turn to ME! Yes, I put you in a situation to turn to Me; but why did I have to make you turn to Me? Why didn't <u>you</u> just turn to Me? Have I been bad with you? Have I? However, your humanity affects your relationship with Me. Stop! - and move forward."

TEACHING on RESILIENCY: REPETITION and RESISTANCE

"Why are you sitting here waiting? Don't you have things that need to be done? Why are you sitting here waiting for Me to speak? Don't you have things to be done? How strange is it to make time for Me on a weekday, wouldn't you say? Shall I be honored? Shall I be pleased? Shall I be grateful? It takes one out of every one hundred people to give Me a moment of their time, in their own time! It takes one out of every one thousand people to reach up to Me in their own time! It takes one out of one million people to seek Me in their own time!

"It takes so much effort to come to Me, but such little effort to stray away: one thought, one temptation, one second to stray away. This is not directed at you, but it is directed at everyone! All it takes is one second to stray away; but days, months, years to return!

"I AM not unforgiving. I AM not angry. I AM not unfaithful. I AM not judgmental. I judge, I rebuke - but I Love. I Love, Child - I Love! My Love covers all other actions and emotions. Yes, I thank you for giving Me time today. I thank you for seeking Me! I thank you for inviting Me into your heart. But I thank you most of all for love! When you love, you accept all My Gifts, My Claims and My Blessings!

"To love Me is to make mistakes, but to come back to Me! To love Me is to sing to Me! To love Me is to pray to Me! To love Me is to invite Me into your heart! To love Me is to enjoy My Presence! To love Me is to let

Me help you, hold you, walk with you, and enjoy all the moments that pass by! By allowing Me to be part of every moment, is allowing Me to enter your life and guide it, rule it and direct it! It is allowing Me to direct you to Me, and ultimately to your Salvation!

"I know you question, you wonder, you doubt, and you pull away. Until you are satisfied with yourself, you will always question what is inside you. There will come a time when you will no longer need to wonder what other people will think about all this - you will just be! Because that is what causes all the doubts, and wondering, and questioning: your feeling of unworthiness, and of what other people will ultimately think. Will you be looked upon as crazy, foolish, or just mentally handicapped? But there is a big part of you that shuns all the words, and all the voices; because you know that I AM, and you are! Hold on to that part! There will come a time when you will be able to stand up to everyone, and everything! You are still growing and learning, and this is all new STILL. Why did I make you bold the word 'still'? It is because, although it has been many months, it is still new for you. You have not fully processed everything that has happened. Child, you are waking up, you are opening your eyes, and you are starting to understand! Do not go back now! Do not turn around, but continue moving forward!"

"Whenever you speak and question, or make statements that are not true, The Father is going to show you the answers, the same way He showed you today. You reminisced how everyone in your life has cheated, or lied, or been unfaithful. The reality is this: the ones that have not, have not entered your life because they were not what you were looking for! When you were looking for honesty, faithfulness and religious, can you say that is what you were offering? How can you expect to receive what you cannot offer?

"There are many faithful followers out there, Child! Remember what I said about positive thinking: this applies to that as well. What you believe is based on your small amount of experience. There are 100,000,000 people out there with just as much experience to share. Yes, the world is not a happy world. Yes, it is full of lies, dishonesty and remorse; but there is a part that smells wonderful, looks angelic, and feels spectacular! What about that part of the world? You dismiss the most important part of existence: the ability to grow, and change, and blossom.

"Look at My People: how many times were they in the dark: black and empty? How many times did they return back to Me and blossom? Look at your own life: you were dark, then you were shining; you became dark, and then light again. It is a process of keeping faith steady, and the only concrete element of your life!

"Why are you thinking I AM all over the place tonight? Don't you see how all this ties to one small, effortless, tiny word? Child, the word is resiliency: repetition and resistance! Resist the enemy, repent of your wrong doings, and fight back!

"When you wake up, you have a routine, don't you? When you start something new, it is hard to follow it until it becomes a routine. Then it is hard to break, right? That is what repetition is: it is the ability to create, and to maintain it. To always seek Me, turn to Me, and love Me is to always have Me on your mind, and heart, and soul! That takes effort and time, and with repetition it becomes natural!

"It takes time to undo the mentality of turning to a human being to save you, and to turn to Me! My People need to turn to Me, not each other: not to doctors, not to money, and certainly not to themselves, which is satanic! No, this is letting the enemy into your life; and having him control everything, without you even being aware of it. For example, your mobile phone is full of the enemy! Why? Because it consumes your energy, time and mind! However, you are not of the mind to think the enemy has such a stronghold on everything around you; but he does!

"That is why, if you have Me in your mind, then the enemy will not be able to control you - even though he has access to your phone. Do you understand? Everything: TV, media, magazines, kitchen - everything, because everything can be turned to sin, negativity, obsession and addiction. Humanity cannot control any of their desires, needs and wants. The enemy controls all this, because he knows the limitation.

"This is My Point, Child. You are used to routine with Me; however, when you do something off-routine, it takes awhile to register and become normal. My approach today has been very different. Why? This is exactly how you think! You jump, and jump, and jump, and jump, and jump. You commit, and jump - and then jump again - and then jump again! How do you expect to follow your own mindset if you cannot sit still? You notice how difficult it is to follow Me, yet you do not notice it is how you think every day!

"I have told you: in order for you to hear, I must show you in your own life. That is the only way you are open to learning. When you experience, you are open to receive; this is just how you function. That is why the enemy has a hold on you; what you experience, you have difficulty letting go. What you experience becomes a solid part of you; however, you must be strong enough, and faithful enough, to fight everything the enemy throws at you!

Whenever you question, ask or say, 'That is not accurate', it will be shown to you. The Lord is with you! The Father is with you! The Father is showing you, guiding you, and directing you! He will show you all that you are missing, but it takes effort and time to return back to Him.

"You cannot understand everything because you do not see everything. You experience what you think and feel is right, and that is what locks

TEMPTATIONS, TRIALS AND TRIBULATIONS

the enemy inside. You have to be strong in your choices and decisions. That means your strength has to lie in Me, and only Me! You can get lost with the masses, or you can choose to direct them. Walking on water is directing everyone to faith and trust! Your desire to be with someone, especially someone who loves Me, is what drew you. But you have to be wiser to realize what people say is not always reality. It is what they desire to be, but reality is much more difficult, and must be persistent, resilient and repetitive. Going to Church every week is repetitive, but it sets a tone to keep you in check. For even if you do not want to attend, you might hear something that will force you to light-the-fire again for Me! Do you understand?

"What I want from you is what you want from Me! You want My Support, Help, Love and Direction. I want your support to support My People. I want your help to guide My People. And I want your love: to love My People, to deliver them, and free them. What you seek from Me, I seek from you! You can change a single person's mind to save them from damnation, and show them My Love and Freedom.

"However, I AM even better than that; for I AM not making you do it on your own! But I AM providing people that will support alongside you! For you cannot see or touch Me, but you can see and touch the people I provide for you. When you choose Me, I have always chosen you; when you love Me, I have always Loved you; and when you return to Me, I AM already there waiting! My People have to understand this! My People have to understand it is not too late; and that there is joy in Salvation, and joy in returning back to Me! Your experiences will help you convey all that you need!

"Remember to sing with the birds, swim with the fish, and lead with the ants. Remember to rise with the sun, and sleep with the moon. Remember to thank and praise Me in all moments: good and bad, happy and sad - especially in moments of anger and hurt, sadness and pain! Never forget to thank Me in the best, happiest and most peaceful moments; for I AM always there in grief and pain. That is when you need Me, so I AM very present! However, in your happiest moment, I AM there too! Remember to thank Me in those days, as well.

"I AM pleased. I AM pleased, but pleased is not enough. Time will reveal all, and time is running low! For now, I AM pleased! Now, why are you sitting here, waiting for Me to speak? There are many things to be done!"

TEACHING on THE HEART and FAITH

"Why waste time? It is so easy to waste time. Do you realize how much time one second is? Do you realize how much time one minute is? Within that one second, you could lose your life, and it would be too late to enter My Gates! Within two seconds, everything can change. Don't waste time, Child; it is very precious. You can only commit with your heart, Child. Your mind will never be stable, but your heart can be. Your words have the power to create. Imagine that power with more faith! Do not promise what is unknown. Promise to have heart, and to have faith!

"I have told you before, My Strength is revealed in your weakness! Speak My Name, seek My Face, and I will give you strength to move forward. Do not be rash in your decisions, Child. You sin in your rash decisions. Your future is bright only if you follow My Path! False promises are tools for the enemy to attack you, and get you into temptation. Child, move forward! I AM here. Seek Me. Seek My Face! I AM present, Child. I will battle with you!

"Shame is of the enemy. Do not feel shame. I told you the weight you put on will be taken off just as easily. Trust My Word, trust My Teaching, and follow My Path. Do not let another moment go by! Your mind and thoughts are in temptation. Seek My Word. Come to Me!

"Your heart is available; now release your mind! I will grant all your desires, Child. I will grant you blessings, but seek Me! I AM waiting, Child! Don't keep Me waiting any longer. Commit! Succeed using My Strength, My Love, and My Blessings.

"Do not look back, Child; look forward. I will bless you! You will wear your clothes, and you will lose more weight. However, follow My Footprint, and I will carry your burdens. Remember this: in weakness, seek My Face, speak My Name, and praise Me!"

TEACHING on GOSSIPPING

"Careful not to become a gossiper. Everyone has faults, but to have the grace to hold it dear to your heart is what sets you apart."

TEACHING on POSITIVE THINKING

"Why have you clouded such negativity inside yourself? Why do you not listen to Me, and move forward? You are stuck, and it is getting deeper. You move one step forward and two steps backward! You need to move forward, Child! It is not too late to move forward and return!

"Positivity is the fuel your mind feeds on. Whenever you think positive, you breathe it in, you absorb it into your blood, and you feel it! It is fuel for your spirit! Negativity is what sucks all the fuel out; it leaves you dry and empty. Positivity is the light and the flow of movement to go ahead. Stop thinking negative! Stop being, and start living again in Me! You must start living again in Me! You cannot drown yourself in negativity.

"These are all lessons for you, and for everyone around you; but only if you come back to Me in order to be able to speak about it. You are not the only one going through such events; but you have Me, and you turn away from Me! Others do not have Me, and thus cannot be helped like you can. What you are going through is difficult, and it will bring

THE LAST MESSAGE

plenty of pain and tears; but you must plow forward! You must speak to Me, and pray to Me like you used to, with your heart and soul! You are disconnected! Remember: positive mind, positive attitude, and positive journey!

"There is nothing negative about your life, Child! There is nothing negative about your events. You made mistakes; and yes, they have repercussions. But it is not negative, Child; it is a growing process! You make everything so grand, Child. Whether it is positive or negative, you choose to make them very big! On some points, it is a very positive trait; but when you get stuck, you force yourself to be stuck!

"Child, don't you see? You have so much potential that the enemy is making useless. You must rise up! You must start thinking positively! <u>There is nothing more positive than My Blood, and what I did for you</u>! But you are so stuck that you cannot seem to move. You asked for strength, and I brought you strength! You asked for My Help, and I brought you My Help! Now you have to accept it, and move forward!

"The dream showed you are cleansed, but you have the choice to accept it or not. If you do not accept it, you choose to wear dark; but if you do, you choose to wear white. The hat was the start, because it was the beginning of you choosing to wear white; your hat made you see the beauty inside you. Negativity sucks everything from your soul, and leaves you dry. The white hat prevails, and is on your head - which is an improvement from not wanting to wear white at all. It is choices, Child! You have asked for cleansing; I provided it. But now, you have to accept it, and move forward.

"TRUST, Child! Have FAITH. Hold My Hand, and move forward. I have told you about the joy waiting for you; but you cannot even hear it, because you are so stuck in negativity. Move forward! Reach out and touch Me! Move forward! Move ahead, Child! There are big changes happening all around you. I told you, weight will come off as easily as it came on. Stop, look up, and think positive! I AM your only Reason for positive thinking. I AM the only Reason to think positively. I AM, therefore you are!

"Therefore, you think positively! You reach for Me, and you praise Me! You claim everything I have to offer, and you look up and say:

'Your Loving Patience has endured all my trials and temptations. But now I can say that I have reached the top with nothing but praises for You - the Only One Who has carried me, picked me up, held me, and loved me.'

"Positivity is the fuel of the spirit. When I was on the mountain, Child, what did I say? 'If it is Your Will, It will be done!' Because I knew that His Will would bring positivity to My Suffering! Knowing I was doing The Father's Will was the only positive outlook I had! It saved you! It could save all! I AM the only reason to be positive! There is no better reason than that:

- "Psalm 62: This sums up everything I have explained to you in this lesson;
- "Deuteronomy 24: It is simple, very simple, how He has saved many with One Hand, and allowed others to be saved from another hand. He has saved you with One Hand, and allowed others to be saved by you with another. He has saved you with One Hand, and allowed others to save you with another. It is the giving and loving nature of The Lord! To do right, you must learn to give. That was your ultimate reason to turn to The Lord. Originally, you wanted to help as you had been helped. Go back to the beginning, Child, and recall. Remember why you wanted to be a Christian - why you chose Me. Go back to your reasoning, and thoughts, and actions, and realize: when you do something with another, then they have the ability to pay it forward, and do it to someone else. You were not only helped with others, but you were helped by The Lord's Hand. And you were helped by your faith, and the support around you.

You have the Gift to help others now in the same way; but you must go back to the beginning, and rekindle all your reasons as to why you chose Me;

- <u>Luke 16</u>: You are an offering, a gift. Whoever cannot accept that, then they are not worthy of the gift. This is to be your line of understanding. A dishonest person will always be dishonest; because they cannot see the gifts all around them, they will try to use everything around them to create 'a gift' for themselves. However, when they cannot see all the gifts around them, they cannot see the blessings The Lord has given them.

"Whoever can be trusted with very little can be trusted with much. Child, The Lord has trusted you with little, which means there is much more to be gifted and learned. If He can trust you with much, imagine what He will reveal to you later! Your spirit He will replenish: your faith, your strength, your courage!

"You have been praying for all these, but not with all your heart and soul. Remember how you used to pray, and how you used to speak to The Lord! Return to that, Child; and return to Him in all your ways: heart, mind, body and soul! Realize that the precious moments and Gifts shared with you will only make sense the day you return to US in spirit:

> 'Remember, He is the only One Who healed you, carried you, lifted you, walked with you, held your hand, medicated you, listened to you, laughed with you, cried with you, and Loved you! He is the Only One Who provided all that and much more, more than you realize! Now, you return to Him and praise Him.'

"The greatest thing in life is to love and be loved in return. <u>The Lord Loves, and the greatest feeling for Him is to be loved in return</u>! Let us rejoice in The Lord, and praise Him for His Patience, Love and Faithfulness."

__TEACHING on THE TIMING TO SPEAK__

"The timing is not right for Me to speak. I cannot reveal much, and you cannot understand yet! I have nothing else to say. Go back to basics: go back to reading The Word. The Word will reveal and answer questions I cannot reveal, for your understanding is limited. I AM always here, but I will not always speak. When I cannot reveal something, I will not speak!"

__TEACHING on RIDDLES, RIDDLES, RIDDLES__

"<u>Read Judith 16</u>: What a great honor it is for those who are called to do My Work! What a great honour for all to see and grow. Such honour is given by The Father - and only The Father - for all His Glory, and His Angels, and for the people to see. To be glorified is a tremendous Gift; however, it is how you see it. To be chosen is to be burdened with responsibility; but is it really a burden, or is it a Gift? What is all this leading to? What will all this come to?

"This Work is not for the weak and weary. This Work is not for the wealthy and comfortable. This Work is not for the perfect; however, it is for the humble and hungry; for the starved and staggered! It is for those who have clung to hope and faith, and who have conquered everything!

"How easy would it have been for Judith to have married and moved forward with her life? How easy would it have been? What are you seeking? What are you craving for? What is your will and desire? None of this matters; for if you are to seek The Father's Work, and be His Person, then none of this matters!

"There will be events happening in a short while. The results will rely on what you have chosen to do. It can go in two directions; which direction it leads to depends on your choice. Where would it lead? How easy it is to proclaim to do His Will, and to be His, and do only His Will; yet

THE LAST MESSAGE

how difficult to conquer such bold statements! How easy to commit yourself to The Father, but how easy to fall and make mistakes. How easy to move forward, but how difficult it will be to move forward if you move backward:

> 'Riddles, riddles, riddles: where will they lead?
> What will happen? Where will you go?
> What will you do? Where will you end up?
> Riddles, riddles, riddles: everything is a riddle.
>
> 'Riddles, riddles, riddles: where will you be?
> What will you do? Where would you go?
> Who would you be? Riddles, riddles, riddles!'

"There are no answers to these except what you choose to do. Then the answer will lead to such cases:

> 'Watch your step! Don't fall in!
> Watch what you wear! Don't fall in!
> What will you do? Don't fall in!

"What AM I talking about, Child? What could it possibly be? Those who have ears to hear, eyes to see, and hearts to love will know the answer! What AM I warning against? Is it an illusion, or is it a reality? Is it something you are seeing, and touching; or is it something make-belief? What are you seeing, Child? Riddles, riddles everywhere!

"<u>Read Acts 16:35 (Paul and Silas are Released from Jail)</u>: Listen carefully, Child. There is a big cost to pay to be My Spokesperson. What you choose to accept and commit to will lead you down a Path from which you cannot return! Riddles are surrounded by demons, and demons are surrounded by satan:

> 'What you cannot control, you indeed can control;
> What you lack, you indeed have;
> What you need, you indeed have.'

"What you lack is provided freely and whole-heartedly. What you wish for is already a reality; but what direction are you going to come from?

> 'Riddles, riddles, everywhere;
> Riddles, riddles, in the air;
> Riddles, riddles, up and down;
> Riddles, riddles, all around!
> Riddles, riddles, why is it so?
> Riddles, riddles, forget your lair;
> Riddles, riddles, no more riddles;
> Riddles, riddles: no more riddles!'

Tired aren't you, Child? It is I doing it! You shall awake soon. Riddles are not bad, Child. But they are not good, either; for you can easily make the foolish choice.

"Read 1 Chronicles 19: All these are riddles, Child! Put the three scriptures together, and see how this pictures a plot where you can make choices. These are all clues to help you understand the riddles. First, the Prophetess, the mighty follower! Then, the battleships; where will you aim? Where will you land? What will be the outcome? Where will you go? Then the victory: whose victory it will be still remains unknown! For all these depend on your choices: to make the right ones!

"Riddles, riddles, riddles . . ."

TEACHING on SILENCE

"I will not come again until you have chosen Me! Seek Me, repent and cleanse! I have nothing further to say."

TEACHING on THE BURNING FIRE of RAGE!

"Stop doubting! I cannot go forward if you continue to doubt. It is very simple: have faith! For when you heal others, you have to believe it before they do. When you believe, you allow the process to begin. If you do not believe, then the process stops with you. They may believe you are My Healer; but if you don't, how can you actually heal them? It is all about what you believe. Do you have the faith to be My Instrument? How else will you tell someone to walk, when they cannot; or tell someone to breathe, when they cannot? You have to have it, so you can pass it along! Remember what I said to you in the past: you have to have the faith, for you are the tool to heal. It is by you that their faith is rejuvenated! You have to believe, and you have to have the faith. This is not something I can help fix. It is on your shoulders, and on you to move forward now. I have physically removed all barriers tying you to the enemy. Now open your eyes, and see clearly, and move forward.

"Jump, Child - and have faith that you will land on your feet, and not on your back. Going forward, it is only My Will, My Path, My Journey, My Direction and My Doing! It is all about what I want, and how I can proceed to help My People; for it is about preparing My People for Salvation!

"I have revealed Myself to you:

- I have been in you;
- You have heard My Voice;
- You have seen My Glory;
- You have seen My Light;
- You have felt My Powers;
- You have felt My Touch;
- You have felt My Anger;
- You have felt My Disappointment;
- You have felt My Distance;
- You have felt My Love;

- You have seen My Healing;
- You have seen Me Save;
- You have seen Me!
- You have seen My Mother;
- You have seen My Father;
- You have felt The Father;
- You have heard The Father.

"You have experienced it all: The Voice, The Presence, The Spirit in all forms! What more is there for you to see? You are too afraid to see Me in the flesh, but one day that will be revealed.

"The Transfiguration is Me in all My Glory, in all My Shapes, in all My Appearances, in all My Voices, in all My Ways. It is ME! You seek Me! You have proof of Me!

"Now seek Me, and go on your way. Have faith, Child. Your new path is just beginning. Wait till you see what is in store for you. You continue your path with Me, and I promise you will have surprises you cannot fathom!"

TEACHING on UNITY, STRENGTH and FAITH

"I AM here! How wonderful it is to come together after a long time. How wonderful it is to gather again. How wonderful it is to share together again! Why has it been so long since we have shared together? Why has it been so long since we have united? What has stopped you from coming and uniting with Me? What was so important that you could not stop and unite with Me?

"My Child, your time will come when you will be ready and capable to teach, love, and live as My Will is for you. For now, you must continue to clean out; and be diligent, and serious for faith like Abraham's, strength like a lion, and love like My Love!

"How wonderful unity is, isn't it? - unity amongst friends, strangers, and followers! Unity is the gathering of minds on a common goal; but when I AM the common Goal, it is not just unity, but Wisdom and Love!

"In unity, one does not fail. Disunity is a big tool for the enemy to use! Have you noticed that the enemy is always lurking around? Do not fear, and battle on! What you experienced today was a little nudge. The more you remain in unity, the stronger you will become.

"I would like you all to think about this, and realize now that we are together: let nothing separate our time together. For apart we are weak, but together we are strong! Apart we are broken, together we are mended! Apart we are tired and at fault, together we rejoice and recharge!

"What does it mean to be united, connected and together? No matter what opposition or difficulty you go through, it is always easier if you rely only on Me. When you are separated, you cannot breathe well, because you cannot see your own faults clearly. United, you will have the Armour of the Holy Spirit to protect you, guide you, and lead you to Me!

"My Word is My Promise! It is My Life! It is My Breath! It is the only Way to Me! I have told you to read My Word. It is not to read to obey, but it is to read to gain Wisdom, and Salvation, and Strength, and Hope, and Love, and Peace. Without My Word, you cannot proceed to help others. Without your Armour, you cannot help others! Without your Sword, you cannot help save and free My People! The Word is your Shield, your Armour, your Weapon and your Sword! It is the Oxygen you need to breathe to live! It is the Heart that pumps the blood to survive! It is everything, and everything needed, to seek My Salvation!

"Read My Word! Do not change My Words: READ MY WORD! Listening to, and watching My Word does not suffice; only reading My Word! To read is to understand, to occupy the eyes: to occupy the visual and auditory imagination. One day, you will be speaking to hundreds of people. How do you expect to teach, and guide, and lead people to freedom, if you cannot quote from the very Being that set you free? My Word is the Password to Life! It is the Secret to Freedom! It is the Food, Water and Air needed to live! Understand?

"Today's lessons are about unity and strength combined - about strength and faith together. It is about relying on My Words to live and lead others. Come back to Me! You are walking back right now. Run back to Me, do not walk! Children, thousands wish to be in your place right now, seeking Me Personally! Run back to Me! You walk, and jog, and stroll; but it is now time to run! Run, I say! Drop everything around you, and run back to Me! I will bless you, and lead you.

"The New Year will be very busy. It will be My Time to gather the flock and feed them: FEED THEM! HARVEST THEM, AND FEED THEM MY FRUIT! I NEED you to be ready, to be ready to feed them My Fruit! Enough time has lapsed, enough time has passed! We are entering a new stage. Run back to Me! Drop all your doings, and return to Me with a vengeance that no enemy can stop!

"My departing Words to you tonight are:

- Unity is strength;
- Unity is love-binding;
- Unity is growing faith;
- Unity is acceptance of wrongdoing, and repentance.

"Together you can see, and hear, and help each other rise up; but knowing that you can only rely on solely Me, and no one else but Me! I will strengthen you united; but apart, you are broken!

"Believing in Magnificence creates Rays of Light! Time is ticking, but it slows down in unity. Next time you feel tired, unite together to build, and share your strength. Unity is fundamental in gaining and sharing

My Spirit, for I AM always present when you are together. Magnificence creates Rays of Light! Let My Light shine through your hardship, and cast Peace in its spot."

TEACHING on REFLECTIONS

"If the spirit does not match external beauty, there is nothing left to shine and reflect. That external beauty is altered, that beauty is shattered, and that beauty is dimmed; but spiritual, inner beauty is sunshine! This beauty is reflected, and this beauty is magnified!

"Each shattered glass of the mirror is symbolic of evil: hatred, anger, disappointment, sadness, revenge, wrath, envy, emptiness, weakness and pride. The more darkness within, the more shattered the reflection will be; the more light within, the more illuminating the reflection will be.

"Beauty is as deep and illuminating as your love: love for Me, My Father, My Work, My People, and YOU! If you cannot love yourself, you cannot accept My Love for you. If you cannot accept My Love, you cannot accept My Work, My Deeds, My Path and My Vision! My Work is Mine, but it is shared with you. My Love is Mine to give, but it is received by you. My Life is Mine to give, and it is received by all!

"All your anger, hurt, shame, disappointment and frustration strive from your lack of faith: your faith to be loved by Me, to be in My Hands, to have My Plan control your life, and to be free in My Will. Letting go of all the above is freedom, Child. Letting go of all the baggage is freedom, Child! The hurt, anger and frustration, the disappointment, sadness and pain will all pass.

"Once your mirror is mended, the light will illuminate. Until then, you are seeing shattered pieces; and they will continue to shatter until you mend them. Your faith in Me and My Promises will mend them! Your faith in My Gifts and my Work will mend them! Don't you see, the mirror is a reflection of your inner beauty?

"'You require nothing, and acquire everything!' Do you understand the impact of such a strong statement? You undermine your strength with Me, combined. You seek strength, and determination, and courage; but you do not realize that this strength is not yours, but Mine; and combined, it is all you seek and need!

"Child, stop feeling so weak; for it is the enemy trying to make you feel so vulnerable. How long have you fasted; and how long have you had the strength, courage and drive to do so? That same strength, courage, and drive has not left you; but you have lost your faith in Me, and thus have felt very weak and broken. It is not easy to fast, Child; and especially for such long periods of time. It is not easy to deny the world, and only follow Me; but you did, and have done so! You must fight, and realize the enemy is blinding your strength; so you only feel and see weakness!

"Each day you must do one thing to take care of yourself; and as you continue, you must add to this treatment. When you reach the end of the week, you will realize how fast the mirror is restored, and how small is the enemy! For this, you must put an effort, every day, to do one thing for yourself; and know that I have given you the strength, courage and thought to do one thing for yourself! By the end of the week, you will have seven things to do for yourself - and realize that your worth, strength and control lay in you, and not the enemy! For you chose to follow Me, and you chose to compete, and you chose to break his stronghold!

"What happened to that angel, the angel with incredible beauty? He fell, and became the most envious and resentful angel of all! His inner beauty finally gave freedom to what he sought after: 'the good'! To have such beauty is to desire the beauty of 'the good'; because for each fallen beauty, his envious hunger is filled: it is one less person for him to envy!

"You are worthy of many blessings, the same blessings the 'illuminator' envies. What he seeks and wants he cannot achieve! But if you fall, and give him more power, he will attain it; and leave you with nothing! That is his goal, Child! Every soul he seeks, he leaves empty and dark; for he takes their beauty and good, and leaves nothing behind. What I own, he seeks. What I bless, he seeks. What I AM, he desires; for he is left empty, broken and dark.

"Do realize this: faith has been around from the beginning of time: Faith, Love, and Mercy. To have the Eternal Love of The Father, to have the Faith to believe in His Eternal Love, and to know and believe in His Mercy - Love brings Mercy on all the souls He Loves. You need to realize just how powerless the enemy is; only your belief in his words has given him power. Everything is possible through The Father, The Lord, and the Friend of all; but nothing is possible without such Faith, Love and Mercy!"

TEACHING on TIME IS TICKING FOR YOU

"Time is ticking for you: tick, tick; tock, tock; tick, tick; tock, tock! How much more time shall I wait? Today you realized how long I have been waiting for you to follow Me! Now that you realize, follow Me! I AM waiting for you to follow Me! Follow Me in blessing, follow Me in joy, follow Me in glory, and follow Me in love!"

TEACHING on DEMONIC OPPRESSION, AND SELF-PUNISHMENT

"I have heard all your apologies. Why can't you hear that I have already washed your sins, and forgiven you? Let go and be free of this, and realize that I have forgiven you! You will make mistakes, and you will grow from them.

"To feel such guilt is purely demonic. Why do you feel such guilt? Don't you realize the burden you are feeling is false guilt? The pain you are feeling is a result of dead weight! All the mistakes and disobedient behavior you have committed has caused these demonic entities to enter and create chaos.

"Instead, I have reached My Hand out to you, waiting for you to grab a strong hold. You are reaching, but you cannot see where My Hand is! You are struggling to see because of all the fog separating your mind and heart. You choose Me, but you do not know how to reach Me! Can't you see? You do not need to reach Me; I AM already here! Clear the fog, and see My Face! See My Arm reaching, and grab it!

"Do not be afraid of the night; do not be afraid of the dark; and do not be afraid of starting a new routine. If you follow My Path, I promise this will be the last downfall you face by yourself. The pain and guilt is at its highest right now. There will be many tears shed. But when all this is done, you will see the beautiful lights and the joy around you once again. One of the hardest lessons for My People to understand and realize is that, even in darkness, I AM Light! And if there is Light, then darkness ceases to exist. One candle can light up the entire sky! Imagine what I can do!

"Do not worry, for you are stronger and mightier than you think. You will go away, and you will see My Beauty! You will feel My Presence, and you will praise and thank Me. You will come back a different person mentally.

"Your time has not come yet to help others, because you cannot bless them without affecting your blessings. The time will come when you will be able to bless many, but it is not now. I will help you, but now is not the time in every aspect: for emotionally you are too weak, financially you are struggling, and to heal you are not ready as you require deliverance yourself. However, the time is coming up, and things will change.

"I have said this before: trust in My Words! Things will change rapidly, the way the sea-waves crash against the shore! The night will fall, the sun rise and a new day dawn."

TEACHING on OUR WILL

"YOU WANT STRENGTH, I GIVE YOU STRENGTH! YOU WANT COURAGE, I GIVE YOU COURAGE! YOU WANT WISDOM, I GIVE YOU WISDOM! REMEMBER, THIS I TELL YOU: you asked for it; I AM giving it to you! NOW claim it, and do not forget that I AM giving it to you! Mark this time; for you will know that in this moment, I have given you what you are seeking! And do not say I did not help you when you asked! From this moment further, I have provided all you need to move forward: to seek, and to move foremost without any attachments from the enemy. Any choice you make will be because it is your choice, and not because I did not provide you with what you are seeking, understand?

"You want strength, I have given you strength! You want courage, I have given you courage! You want wisdom, I have given you wisdom! What else is there that you seek? There are many changes that will happen very quickly, but it has not started yet as there are some things that need to be revealed and revised. So much time has been wasted with disobedience!

"The only ties that should be kept are Mine, and only Mine! When you are fully Mine, then you can fully follow My Work and My Voice! When you choose Me first, you have the ability to be free in the Spirit, to follow anything I say! Only when you are truly free in the spirit will you hear and follow. When your mind is clear, and your heart is free, there is only One Voice, and One Action you follow: Mine! When there are many strongholds, then it is difficult to hear and see.

"Only when you are Mine can I lead and control your paths and life. When you do not surrender to Me, then I cannot lead and guide you. I can use you to change many people's paths only when you are truly Mine. I have the ability to speak through you in a loving, gentle and calm manner. By using people's experiences to convey change, you can point them in My Direction to do My Will!"

TEACHING on "YOU REAP WHAT YOU SOW"

"The message is very clear: you reap what you sow! So remember, in all your actions you have reactions: what you do has a reaction. You see, Child, the effort you put into getting to know Me is not the same as you receive back: it is more than you can even imagine!

"You take one step forward, I take ten. My Arms are wide open! I will help you in Comfort; but you must continue to put in an effort."

TEACHING on FAITH and OBEDIENCE

"You do not have to always understand everything; you just need to learn to obey without question. Sometimes the best surprises happen when you do not realize it. Obey Me, and you will be overjoyed! Stop asking questions! Follow the Path I have laid out for you day-by-day. Follow My Path! You will know when you are falling off it.

"I will prove it! *Open The Word to Mark 5*: 'Jesus heals the possessed man'. Your story is one of testimony: your testimony is your experience and path. What path you choose to take will result in an outcome of your doing. Money is just paper, but faith is ecclesiastical! So why would you worry about paper? Paper is useless, it will burn; but faith cannot burn, and faith will make you blossom.

"As long as you are open, I can use you greatly as a Messenger; but you need to work on your issues with faith:

- Continue moving forward;
- Be careful who you speak to regarding this topic of faith;
- It is a journey to follow Me, but one that requires a lot of faith: a lot of blind faith!

"*Open The Word to Joshua 22*: Witnesses: that is the key! To have faith to stand and say, 'I believe blindly' is a gift. Remember to be grateful, and remember to thank Me. I cannot do it all on My Own: I need your cooperation. Trust Me! You are just human, but are a channel and funnel used to share My Messages, and direct others to My Thoughts. I will help you."

TEACHING on "MY LOVE HAS FILLED YOUR HEART"

"One of the most beautiful and rewarding features of patience is the welcome back! Freedom is not what you seek as a human, but what your soul seeks within My World! You continue to state that you want to be free, and you are returning 'Home'; however, these statements are inaccurate. It is a matter of obedience and self-control.

"You still have not fully returned, but you are getting closer and closer. Oh Child, the blessings awaiting for you once you return! What you have experienced will be the most important lesson you will teach, for it is a lesson of life and death in the spirit. Just as easily, you could have lost your life; for the spirit weakens and dies, and no longer has the faith to fight and choose to live with Me. It gives up and surrenders to the world, and forfeits its standing for Salvation. When the spirit awakes, nothing can stop it from blossoming; but a broken spirit will cause fatal destruction.

"What you see as romance and love is so little to what real Love and Romance is! What you seek does not compare to what exists! What you choose for yourself is so small and finite that, once you receive a taste of reality, you will laugh off the concept of 'love and romance'! The Love

TEMPTATIONS, TRIALS AND TRIBULATIONS

spoken and the Love read in The Word is timeless! The love you have seen and spoken of is momentary. How can you compare the two? Do you realize you have been holding on to the momentary?

"Dance, sing, rejoice in your spirit. Do not be afraid to dance and sing. Yes, it has been a year since you began this journey; however, this month will finally lead you to completion. Forget everything worldly, and rely only on Me! I promise you the same I have always promised: I will grant you blessings you will not be able to forget. Do not think you are the only one I bless: I bless all My Children, but some have greater roles than others, and some have more significant roles than others. You disobeyed severely, yet The Father still blessed you with His Patient Love! Do you see the difference between your love and Mine?

"Do you think the person I bring into your life will have the same Love? If it is My choosing, then yes; but if it is your choosing, then you have set yourself up for sorrow. What you have considered to be love to this point, and what you will learn to be real Love, does not compare; and you still will not understand until you experience it!

"Yesterday you declared you want someone to pray with, to go to Church with, to walk in the same faith with you, to grow with you, to Love Me before you, to put Me before all, and to be living in Truth. That is the key; that is what you have sought for so long! So how can you say you were 'in-love' with someone who did not possess these qualities?

"The worst and best thing the enemy has control over is love; for it is not real love, but created love. I AM the definition of Love. I AM Love! What does the enemy want more than anything else? To be ME! To be Love! His version of love is tainted, and will ALWAYS COME APART! My Version, even in death, does not come apart. Love is eternal, and lasting, and never subsides. It is the one thing that lasts forever and ever. Even when you come to Me, it is still standing! But the enemy's love breaks within a fiber of a second (fiber optics). That is why marriages are not stable; because it is all controlled by the enemy. It is not controlled by Me! Child, your mate will be the next one in line; but that will take some time until you are ready, until you are healed.

"The closest relation you have to Love is the love of your pet birds; but even that is limited for you, as you do not know how to express My kind of Everlasting Love. Many people share the same problem as you for many do not know how wonderful, freeing, and Holy this kind of Everlasting Love can be. The ones who know The Father have an understanding of that type of Love, for the only Person who can teach you that Love is Him!

"Come back! I will carry you Myself, and take away your burdens. It will not be easy for you; however, if it was easy, then I would not need your service and love. You often think there are better, more suitable people out there to do My Work; but it is not your choice to decide if you are suitable or not. Remember, your imperfections will become great teaching tools for the future! Stand up straight! Keep your head up, and pray! Pray for understanding of what it truly means to Love! Pray for support, and what it truly means to support one another. And finally, pray for patience: patience to forgive and love in all situations.

"Your love song to Me is touching and loving! However, I want you to sing it once you are completely back. Then it will be the utmost magnificent gift! I have one request of you: stop and think, and then choose and think; and then stop and rethink, and choose and rethink; then proceed. Go ahead and stop thinking, but remember to rethink your decision twice over! Then your final decision will be final.

"Do not look back, look forward! Look ahead. Look at Me! I will bring you back to Me: in My Light, in My Word, and in My Presence! Your figure, your weight, your struggles, your faith, your finances, your life, your friends, your family - all will disappear one day. But I will remain as I AM today, tomorrow, yesterday, and forever! So do not look back! Look ahead to a time where you cannot even imagine; and know that

I have already imagined it for you, before time even began! I will bring you with Me and carry you on My Shoulders, and let you feel light!

"Let us do this again, shall we? Child, continue being patient with your work, as I AM patient with you. Go off, work out, and read My Word. I speak in opening My Word. But it is important to read The Word by the Book also, because you need to know My Story! And do not skip out on the boring stuff, Child! It is boring, but it is how you came to be!"

<u>TEACHING on JESUS' LOVE</u>

"Child, Child, Child! Why are you so afraid? What have I ever done to cause you to fear? I will not put you in a situation to bring you fear! Why do you assume the worst, Child? Why do you assume the worst? Haven't I shown you Love? Haven't I shown you Peace? Haven't I shown you Tenderness? Why are you afraid? Neither satan nor his demons can touch you! I will not put you in harm, nor will I leave your side! I AM always with you! Do not fear!

"Anything I show you is for your benefit. It is to make you stronger. Do not fear, for I will not abandon you or leave you behind. You do not even know what I want to show you! How do you know it is not a blessing? How do you know it is not positive? Just because I said I want to show you things, you assume I will show you terrible things!

"Yes, you need to 'wake up', but fear is not the right way to wake up! When I say, 'Wake up!' I mean realize all you have, all you can do, and all you will do! How do you know I will not show you miracles and glory? Why do you assume I will show you demons and hell? Haven't I said before I will never take you there? How easily you forget! I know My Children, and I know their limitations. When and what I choose to reveal to you is for your blessing and benefit! It is for The Father's Glory, but also for your good! Relax, Child! Relax! Your fear is because of your experience in the past! That will never happen again. Relax! Nothing and no one will come near you!

"I want to show you My Glory! I want to reveal Myself to you, but in a way you will not fear Me. I AM Great! I AM everything and anything you can imagine Me to be! I AM Love. I AM Happiness. I AM Joy. I AM Peace. I AM Tenderness. I AM Kindness. I AM Me! I AM all of the above. Do not fear Me! It is not Me you are afraid of, but the unknown. Unknown is beautiful: unknown is stunning, unknown is glorious, unknown is unimaginable, unknown is reality!

"I love you dearly, but I cannot prepare your way. You must help Me to help you by accepting My Love and Comfort. Can't you see the enemy does not want you to succeed? Can't you see the enemy does not want Me to be revealed to you? Can't you see that is why you are filled with fear? It is so easy to turn away and stand tall, for I AM always with you! I will neither hurt you, nor will I ever leave you. My 'punishment' is not so childish! If I were to punish you:

- I would not use the term 'punish';
- I would 'discipline' with Love.

"Remember all the dreams you have had: did they frighten you? Were you abandoned? Were you left alone? Child, I AM promising you glory! Relax, relax, and relax! Breathe deep, and know it is okay! It is okay for you to feel fear; but it is not okay to let it control you, or to take away your peace or sleep. We are not going to repeat this cycle again! You realize I AM in your room right now! You realize I AM in you right now! You realize I AM all around your house right now! You realize I AM with you right now! Do you realize that I AM already, and have been, and will be! If you know that already, then relax, breathe, and control your mind to destroy all thoughts of the enemy.

"I will not show you hell. I will not show you demons. I will show you things you will not like; but I will also show you things you will love.

You need to realize how serious the enemy attacks are; but that does not mean I will show you demons, or hell, or satan! There is plenty of evil around you in this world that I can show you. Relax, it will not be now! It will be when I choose to show you, but you do not have to worry for now. Just find peace in My Presence, and in My Love!

"I see you relaxing. See the care and love I AM showing you by loving you? If I was the 'God' you perceive, would I show you My Love, or would I let you be in fear?"

TEACHING on AVOIDING TEMPTATION ALTOGETHER

"A tree stock begins thick and sturdy. As time wears on, it becomes twigged, splintered and weakened. When you start, do not succumb to small temptations here and there; for the splintered wood weakens, and has higher possibilities of falling.

"Lesson: if you can avoid temptation, do so altogether! Otherwise, shavings will weaken the core, and cause it to fall. Careful with temptation, as it is easy to fall when you think you are strong. Be more cautious, so you can see your enemies' attack; and not feel grounded, so as to think they will not attack."

TEACHING on "I GIVE IN BLESSING, and TAKE AWAY IN FURY!"

"Commit your time to the project at hand, and make it a top priority; so when you are questioned, your response is not in vain. It is so vital to sleep earlier, because this can become a big problem. Do not think twice about the new changes, for your patience will have paid off; but in doing so, do not get proud.

"It is very easy to get proud! As easy as the blessing was given, it can be taken away! Remember, I have given, and I shall take. What I give, I give in blessing; but what I take away, I will take away in fury! This is not a warning, but a statement to think about. Changes will be happening. Just trust Me, and praise Me. Do not get proud! This I repeat! Do not think twice, but learn to continue to walk blindly in faith. All things may appear one way, but will show up as another. So trust Me; and know that I AM behind, in front, and around you!

"I do not caution you on pride, but I advise you to keep it in your thoughts: pride, not of accomplishments, but of popularity. Just continue doing as you are, and remember to keep My Words in motion. Use My Words in your daily walk. You see, as you grow in Me, I will bless you mightily! It is I Who bless you, but you are following The Father's Journey! Why is this important? If everyone followed The Father's Journey, they too would be blessed! This job is exciting and wonderful; but if it was not for your best interest, The Father would not have allowed forward movement. Do not test Him or His Words, just trust Him!"

TEACHING on A SEASON FOR EVERY TIME

"Child, there is a season for every time. As seasons change, so does time. You have three months to completely change ALL your life! You will only get this opportunity ONCE: never again will it be offered! What you expect and imagine are droppings compared to the changes to come!"

TEACHING on REMAINING SWEET BUT THIRSTY

"How sweet the sound of a new born. How sweet the melody of new life. How sweet the scent of new beginnings. Sweetness is a gift from Me, as is bitterness. 'Sweet' is easy to turn to bitterness. Too much sweetness becomes too bitter! No matter how much sugar you add to bitterness, it will remain bitter! My Path is not always sweet; often you will experience bitterness. Do not think it is a way of life, but a choice you have taken: bitterness is a lesson, it is a gift, and it is a method of coping.

"Why AM I talking about bitterness? Your path is very sweet right now. Do not lead your own way; for the sweetness can turn very bitter! Your path is very sweet, sweet like honey. Keep it sweet! Do not stray!

"I AM baking a cake. The ground level is baked; now let us start with level two. Continue to spend time with Me; I will make My Presence more obvious. Continue to read. I will make more changes. I caution you: do not make this path bitter! TOO MUCH SUGAR WILL MAKE IT BITTER; REMAIN SWEET BUT THIRSTY!"

TEACHING on "I HEAR YOU SPEAK!"

"I hear you speak, but I need you to hear My Words! I need you to eat My Words! The Holy Spirit will rejoice within you, and you will feel My Strength, and My Love and Peace! My Words are your fruits. They are your blessings and wisdom. I will take care of My People, if they are obedient with Me.

"I promise you, Child! I promise you, Child! You commit to fasting and obedience, and I will not only fit you in that dress, but it will be very loose on you! I AM promising this to you! Work out three times a week, and fast. No more hot chocolate, just your shakes. Read My Word! Spend time with Me, and see how skinny you will become! All your clothes in your closet will be loose! I promise this to you! You need to watch and be amazed, Child. Amazed!!! All your desires will be fulfilled, and then some! You saw the aspect of your job! This, Child, is only the beginning! I have big, big plans for you! This job will grow and expand, and you will see to where, and to what heights, I will lift you!

"Wait, and clear your mind of negative thoughts! Clear your mind of foolish thoughts, and focus on My Words - My Words and My

THE LAST MESSAGE

Blessings! You see, Child, many would love to have Me answer them the WAY I answer you! But you have a very special gift: a job to let the world see Me, and get to know Me! I AM here!!! I AM very much alive, and I AM present! I love all My Children! I wait and sit eagerly for one to open the door and accept Me, to accept My Salvation, to accept My Love! You are a Voice for Me! Your sins are sins of many, and your emotions are emotions of many; but, Child, your desires are Mine! They will be fulfilled! Do not worry; for your debts will be wiped! I will erase them! This you will wait to see; but patience is necessary. Do not worry about this. Keep an open eye on Me, only Me!

"I love you. But if you do not obey, The Father will remove all His Blessings, and everything will rot! Everything will rot! This I also promise you: everything positive will become sour and bitter; and you will be left empty, cold, and destroyed! The enemy will consume you, and you will spend your eternity burning!

"This I also promise you: choose My Path, and let Me bless you! Start right now! Love Me more than anything! I will speak My Words to you. Just listen!"

TEACHING on RETALIATION: AS CRUEL AS REVENGE!

"Have I been revengeful with you, or have I retaliated? Why would you behave in such a manner? I teach with love and gentleness! Your lovely bird seeks your attention and love. This is an example of how you should not behave.

"You can be effective in many different ways; do not choose the easy route to attain what you desire. It is not the best method, for 'easy' usually is 'ungodly'. Learn to love with discipline: a gentler voice, a caring touch, a loving approach. Steer clear of impulsive, quick, and easy reproaches. Your pets depend on you; you are their guide; you show them love. Is this how you want them to react?

"Is this how you want Me to react with you? This behavior is disappointing, for it shows no mercy - and the amount of mercy I have shown you! It is time to unlearn such behavior, and follow My Example! My Teaching should prevail. In loving kindness, you will prevail. In harshness and intemperance, you will fail!

"To love and be gentle is more effective than hardness and harshness. If I react the way people generally do, My Heavens will remain empty! Seek My Patience, seek My Love; but most of all seek My Heart! This is a time of mourning and repentance. Strive to reach a new level of sight and sacrifice.

"Do not seek to understand and know everything; I will not reveal them to you. You must follow in blind faith and trust; for you will not always know everything. When I warn you, or reveal blessings to come, it is out of love and compassion; but when I do not, it is to teach or protect! From this point onwards, do not ask to know. When it is important for you to know, haven't I given you the information prior to the time?

"It is in Faith that you learn Wisdom, and in Wisdom that you learn Teaching, and in Teaching that you learn Discipline; and in Discipline you learn the Fear of The Lord!"

TEACHING on DISCIPLINE TO MAINTAIN OBEDIENCE

"This is what you have to understand: My Way is the Only Way! My Teachings are the Only Path! My Standard is discipline! Discipline cuts off the enemy. Discipline is obedience! You are obedient, which makes you disciplined, which allows for My Help, which grants you blessings, which allows for you to continue to be obedient - and thus creates a full circle of harmony! A small crack is all it takes for disorganizations and chaos to enter. Discipline is mandatory, for I AM King; and the King knows what is best!

"It is not a matter of you having a date or a fig here or there, when you are required to fast. It is a matter of you tasting, and allowing temptation to creep in. At the same time, it is not an issue of disciplining yourself to rely solely on Me, but to maintain the ability to be obedient and willing.

"It is a very, very difficult way of living! But what you are seeking, and desiring, and searching for requires such severe discipline and obedience that you must teach yourself starting now! It is so important to learn such loving discipline, for this is how you will learn to teach your children. How many people can say they know true Discipleship? But this is what it takes to reach that level! It is an honor and a privilege to join such a league! I have recruited many, many; but as you are aware, not many respond. However, their fate is sealed, as is yours."

TEACHING on KEYS TO GRATITUDE

"I AM going to tell you a little story . . . a little story . . . a little story . . . ! Lie down, close your eyes, and imagine:

> 'Imagine light so bright, you cannot see anything else but the haze; light so bright, it shines and shimmers; light so bright, it blinds!
>
> 'Now imagine the light with a few streaks in it, dividing the light into little pathways, and streets, and sections. Imagine the light moving along the divisions. What happens now with the light? Is it shining as brightly? Is it as large? With the pathways, what you see is all the mistakes, turnarounds and lessons.'
>
> "You are white, bright and shimmering. You have plenty of pathways that create divisions and separations; however, you are still bright light. With the divisions,

there is a process to mend the broken; but there is also the ability to shine brighter, and move ahead. Eventually, the separations will disappear, and the whole complexity will become simple and overpowering - will overflow the darkness!

"I know you are repentant. I know you are sorry. I know you feel weak. I know you are broken. If you were none of those, would you seek Me? Would you need Me? Your issue is not to be repentant or weak. It is to realize you are great, and full of strength with Me! What you struggle with is very simple to overcome. It is very easy to overcome temptation.

"Step one, I have already given you. It is the ultimate form of defiance to the enemy! Take a decision, and show the enemy how strong you are. Not because you have strength, but because you have asked for My Strength, My Help and My Power to drive ahead! Remember, your future is ahead of you, bright and full of glory; but the enemy does not want to see you move ahead.

"If you continue in this train wreck, you will reach nowhere. It is a train wreck because it only goes in circles. Don't you see? The Father sees everything! He knows everything! He knows you sin and make mistakes! He knows you fail, and you have difficulty getting up; but what you do not comprehend is that He helps you get up, repent, and let go!

"What you see is not colors but lights, Child. You see energy: yellow, red, purple, blue - all these are energy. What you see is what everyone truly is in their form. But how you see it is by My Energy: how I enter, react, and flow through you. You see Me with the Blue Light;

however, it is not always blue. It is shades of blue, aqua, and lavender. When you see blue, you associate it with My Presence; because that is My Form in the Holy Spirit.

"When you promise, you fail. However, when you acknowledge your short-comings and ask for My Help, I AM here to help you. I will heal you! Healing is yellow; healing is golden! Child, I accept your commitment, because it is your way of holding onto Me. It is not your commitment I AM seeking, but your choices to do My Will!

"My Will is not for you to fast, but it is to get you to a place of joy and peace with Me: to get you to a place of unity with Me. The more you are diligent in fasting, the more I can show you, and teach you, and cleanse you. It is not just a rule to fast to get closer to Me, but it is the only way to truly allow Me to cleanse you! You realize you do not need anything of the earth to survive, but just My Love, and Power, and Faith!

"I want you to wake up every morning saying, "I trust You, Father!", and continue repeating that; for your trust is shaken. Not because you do not have faith in Me, but because you doubt being worthy to be picked by The Father. It is not you who chooses to be worthy. You sin, you repent, and you repeat the cycle. You will always sin, and you will always repent; that is why you are human, and that is why I have created Gifts in people like you, to help others find clarity. Why else would The Father gift His children, if not for the purpose of bringing them closer to Me? Otherwise, you would not need to pray to The Father. You would not need acceptance, you

TEMPTATIONS, TRIALS AND TRIBULATIONS

would not need, period; because you would be living for the moment, and not held accountable for your actions.

"I see you as great, fearless, and devout; but that comes from all the lessons and hardships you have learned, experienced, and struggled through. You are great because of your love and commitment to The Father. You are fearless because you have experienced the enemy, and faced his wrath! You have seen, felt, and lived in terror; but have conquered it! You are devout because you will not give up, and you will fight: fight to win the battle. So now, do not give up, but fight! Fight to conquer! I have promised you many, many blessings; but these blessings cannot be revealed until you stop shutting the door on one! One door closes to make way for another. It is not a door we speak of, but life choices: to change direction, do u-turns, or dives.

"I hear your plea, I hear your voice, and I hear your misery. Now hear My Plea; now hear My Voice, and My Joy! Forget what is past, what is in the future; and live right now, this second, for Me! Instead of wondering how the day will be, and about the hardships you will have to conquer, live for the moment in My Work and Will! Just focus on My Will for only this moment, Child! Not for two hours from now, or tomorrow, but this moment! When temptation creeps up, just focus on Me for only that moment! Cast the enemy, and say, 'For this moment, I cast you out!' Then the next moment, repeat it again, 'For this moment, I cast you out, satan!' And again . . . Do not see it as a day's struggle, but as a moment-by-moment struggle! It is much easier to deal with the moment than the hour. It is much easier to deal with the seconds than the minutes. So, focus on each second of the struggle, and conquer that second!

THE LAST MESSAGE

"If there are 24 hours in a day, imagine how many moments you can conquer, and add to your belt of triumph. And imagine how easy it is to conquer that moment! Do not view it as a day, in which you have to climb and conquer the mountain! You have 24 hours to climb, and conquer, and depart. That is a long time, Child! However, you have one day to turn your choices around. See how much more difficult it sounds to clump your time to one day, instead of just hours, minutes and seconds?

"The struggles will come moment after moment, but you will deal with them as that: a fleeting, vanishing, small moment. A struggle and obstacle become so light and easy to say, 'No' to; rather than to chuck up your entire day into wrong-doing and failure! At the same time, if you happen to fail, it is for that moment only, Child! It is not for the whole day or remainder of the day; just for that moment, that second! You can stop, and you can repent; but it is just for that moment!

"I will not weigh you down more than you are capable of lifting; even then, you are not the one lifting, but I AM. In saying this, realize you can overcome! Guilt is empty, but very heavy. When people carry false guilt around, it is very meaningless, and it is obsolete because guilt is not meant to weight you down, and fill you with remorse. It is to let you know in your heart that you did something wrong! You need to stop, back up, reverse, and understand that you did something wrong; and most importantly, to let it go! Without guilt, you do not have the ability to know when you are heading in the wrong direction; or when you have done something wrong, negative, or against My Will! But with guilt, you can turn it around, move in My Direction, and change it to gratitude!

"So, Child, stop going around in circles! For you have a straight, clean path ahead of you!"

TEACHING on A PEACEFUL MIND

"Shhh! Sometimes all you need is some peace. Let your mind relax. Let your mind be calm. Let your mind be still. I do not do things because I choose to do them, but because it is given to Me! The way you follow Me, I too follow My Father!

"Your mind is filled with tremendous amounts of empty noise and clutter. Clear out your mind, and debrief. Allow peace to be with you, and in you!"

TEACHING on THE LORD'S TIREDNESS!

> *"'I AM so tired! I AM so tired! Give ME some water! How terrible it is to be so tired: so tired you cannot think, so tired you cannot walk, so tired you cannot move: exhaustion takes over. I AM so tired! It is nearly over, it is nearly finished. I will soon be with My Father. I AM so tired; but My Tiredness is not physical! My Tiredness has consumed My Every Thought. There is so much responsibility, and there is so much suffering; how can I endure? If it were not for My Father ... I AM willing and ready; but if My Eyes are not on Him, I cannot take another step. It is nearly finished ... !'*

"The last few steps are the most difficult, for you are very tired and very thirsty; but the time is near for it to be finished.

"What does this mean? When you see someone committed and faithful, you do not always believe they are on the right path. Faith to let Me take over and maneuver takes more effort than you taking charge and direction of your own life! As you allow others to see how you have given up control, you allow others to be blessed! It is very simple to have faith to allow Me to take charge; but when it comes to your own desires, it becomes very difficult!

"The time is just around the corner when I will show My People how I have fulfilled My Promises! But only then will they be in awe, and turn to Me! Don't you see? The Father will use you to rise Himself up in His People! In doing so, you will be blessed beyond your imagination, which you are starting to see.

"It is going to be a lot busier soon. You will be pulled in many different directions, but where you will focus is up to you! I will bring many people to your circle. How will you deal with this change? Every single moment, you have the opportunity to make a choice. Even when you do not make a choice, it is a moment you made the choice not to make a choice! Every moment is a lesson, a choice and a thought!

"You see the same way you look at certain people, the same way others will look at you and your life! You see a life of worship in people, and you desire that same life for yourself as others will look at your life, and desire the same for themselves in their lives. It is a circle, an on-going circle! The Father uses people to bring others into His Circle; then, in turn, He uses the same people He brought into the Circle to help others! It is a Circle of Communication: for one person's life changes, and allows that person to change other people's lives - and it continues forward. That way, the more you are faithful, the more effective you are to others - and the more effective others will be with their people, and so on and so forth.

"Why AM I so tired? I AM tired because I AM expressing what it is I felt, and what it was that helped Me carry on: knowing this would soon be over, and I would light up the sky with My over-bearing Responsibility! In doing so, I found freedom in My Father, and I found escape in My Father! And in doing so, I left feeling complete! In doing so, I have saved you thousands of times! I have saved My People hundreds-of-thousands of times! I have saved My People from demise! I have saved My People, and shown them what My Love consisted of.

> *'I AM tired! I AM thirsty! I AM very tired! But soon enough, My Tiredness will cease! And I will be full of rage, and Justice will prevail!!! I AM Tired, I AM very Tired!'*

"But My Tiredness will give many people opportunity to return to Me, and help energize Me! For each person who returns is an extra hand to help carry My Cross! And the more people who return, the less burdened I feel! You are standing near the corner. All you have to do is turn! That is how close you are! Remember, every single moment is a choice, and every single choice has a repercussion. I AM not warning you, but I AM advising you just how close you are, and just how important it is to make every moment count! Now do you understand My Dream? You realized, by your own choice, the importance of repentance, for I was coming! But it is not the time, as The Father has not declared it!"

TEACHING on "I AM HERE, WAITING FOR YOU TO COME MY WAY!"

"Repent of all your sins, and be thankful! You do not always know everything that goes on, but I do. You do not see everything as I do. Some things you do not discover until it is in the right moment. You have seen all My Promises have been accomplished, even in your disobedience! I AM a loving God!

"Now that you are seeing facts, you can start to grow your faith further. You must stop, and thank Me; however, not in remorse but in gratitude!

Do not feel ashamed, for shame is what the enemy wants you to feel; but feel gratitude, and repent. In this moment, you have realized My Goodness. You have realized My Love; and that My Word is honest, and unchanging!

"When people sin, they are the ones that change their paths, not Me! It is not you who needs to prove to Me your worth, but it is you who needs to love Me by obeying Me! I often do things for My Children that they are not aware of. If you were to know everything, what good would it do for you? You cannot see the bad, thus you cannot see all the good. I protect in many situations and ways. I bless in many situations and ways. Because you cannot see it does not mean I AM distant, or that I AM not present! You are fortunate; you were able to see. But what you have seen is but a scratch! What would you do if you saw all that I have done for you?

"My intention of you finding out My Blessings yesterday was for two purposes:

- To show your friend My power and blessings; and
- To make you realize what I say is reality, and that faith is all you need to walk by Me and trust Me.

"I will bless you, but you have to believe that. What you have been struggling with is lack of trust and faith: not in My Presence, but in My Ability to take care of you! You seem to believe you are not worthy of attaining My Blessings; but you are worthy of them, if you obey and follow Me! Do not be surprised at what I have done, because what is to come is much bigger and better. Do not be taken back by someone doing something good for you.

"Repent for your mistakes, repent for your actions, and repent for your sins! And then be grateful for such a loving God Who will love you and bless you. Repent for shame and embarrassment, and realize I want you to feel grateful and blessed! How many people do you think realize I bless them? How many people do you think hear My Promises, and then see them blossom? How many people do you think see just how great My Love is for them? You have such a fortunate blessing! Realize this, and know that there will be more positive blessings to come! Once you can claim these blessings, and accept them; you can allow yourself to choose My Will, and move forward. This is a lesson for you to realize you are worthy to receive blessings, and it is ongoing.

"Many times, My Children do not feel they have 'luck'. It is not 'luck' that they are missing, but faith in My Ability to bless them. It is not luck; but it is faith, obedience, and love. Faith, Child! It is called Faith and Trust! Grow in My Faith, and not what you have been accustomed to. Realize the power of Love and Forgiveness. You love and forgive! You allow yourself to move in a forward direction! Forgive yourself for your foolish ways. Set your mind on Me, and watch what a transformation will come about! Now that you know I have kept My Word in My Blessings, you have to grow your faith and trust in My Ability to Love you and bless you.

"I gave My Own Son for your deliberate disobedience! Don't you think that is a greater Sacrifice? My Love is greater than sin. My Love is greater than deliberate sin!"

TEACHING on "THE LORD COMES! GET READY FOR MY WORK!"

"When I come, I SPEAK! I SPEAK! You have to relax and stop fighting it! It is very difficult to speak when you are fighting! You have to relax!

"Links are meant to be broken; they are part of a whole chain. Links bring chains together. Get rid of ALL links associated. Get rid of ALL links associated, for they will be tied together in chains.

"You will be jumping. Be careful in your landing. You will be jumping. Remember to have steady feet when you jump. Do not be too eager, excited, or anxious - but steady!

"Get ready to go. It is coming up! Will you be ready to go? Get ready. Prepare yourself! Get ready to go!

"Ready? When you can answer that, you will be ready. Prepare yourself! Get ready! My Work! Get ready!"

TEACHING on BELIEVE! EVERYTHING IS POSSIBLE, and NOTHING IS IMPOSSIBLE!

"Child, if I wanted to, I could do it right now! I can do anything at any given moment! You just have to believe, and it can be done! It is so simple! The concept is to believe and have faith! Everything and anything CAN be done if you just believe! I cannot express to you how simple it is! How simple it is! HOW SIMPLE IT IS! It is so incredibly simple! Just believe, and it can be done! Faith grows hair when there is none; faith grows new cells when all are deceased; faith gives seed for a child to grow, feed and come to life! Faith is the invisible cord that is attached to Me, as a baby is attached to its mother by an umbilical cord! It is the same concept, Child! Believe, and it can be done!

"Why can you not see just how fortunate you are? You believe it with all your heart, and it can be done! You will it, and it can be done! You have the ability to pray, and be heard by many. All that you are missing is to understand that the veil between My World and yours is meshed, which means: you have the ability to do in My World and in yours, as I have. There are many with similar gifts, but all different in their own way.

"You plant a seed and water it. It takes faith to believe it will grow, and produce fruit. The same way you have faith that it will grow and produce fruit is how this situation is; you have faith, and your faith will produce and grow fruit for many. You have faith, and faith will lead the way!

"The power to believe without any doubt is the power to perform any type of miracle. What you need to understand is that it is not YOU that will perform it, but I using YOU as a vessel! It is not YOU that can heal, but I that can heal! It is not YOU that can cast out demons, but I that can cast out! It is I-in-you, and not you-in-you!

"What I want you to do this entire week is: pray to believe, and believe it can be done! Starting with your own weight, believe I can do a miracle, and believe it can be done! Learn to BELIEVE I can do anything, at any moment! Do not be afraid to see Me, for I AM all Love. Love is not something to be afraid of! Do not be afraid to be in My Presence; for I AM all Love, and Love is not something to be afraid of! Do not be afraid to be in the supernatural; for it is reality, and reality is great! I have promised you three miracles before your friend's wedding. You will see three miracles happen, and you will be the one to be in awe! You will, and you will believe!

"Envision a sheer liner between where you are, and where I AM. This liner is nothing but invisible! What does this mean? Both worlds are one; but I can see both, and you can see one. I AM telling you, you are in both worlds; but you must believe to be able to do what I seek! It is a beautiful moment to know your faith can move a pebble, your faith can heal a bone, and your faith can do anything - because it is Me doing so in your faith!

"You are chosen for this purpose, which means it is in your calling to do so. As The Father decided to bear all sins and forgive His People, He too decides what roles we must play. And your role was chosen for you, to bring people back to Him! This is a beautiful Blessing! Just believe that it can be done, and it will be done. It is so minor, but so great! Many have faith unshakable, but their calling is different. Many have faith, and seek to find more; but their Path is different. We all share the same

Path to The Father. As I had to follow My Path and bear all stains, you must follow your Path in choice, faith and love!

"What you take from this lesson is that nothing is impossible, and all is possible: all forms of healings, miracles, and Gifts of the Spirit. Stay on track, and you will show everyone what faith can do!"

TEACHING on "I AM HERE!"

"I AM here, I AM here; I AM here!
I AM here, I AM here; I AM here!
I AM here, I AM here; I AM here!
I AM here, I AM here; I AM here!
Here I AM! I AM here! I AM here!

"When you go home, you put on the dress and see what I have done! This is a work in progress, and it will take a few days to be finished.

Do not wear your glasses; do NOT wear them! What you have asked for, I have done! It too will take some time to adjust and be cleared. It takes time, because faith has to be grown with this. Now that you have experienced some changes and healing, you can grow your faith to complete the task! Have faith, and all is possible! Just watch and see what I AM capable of doing!

"I will use you for tremendous healing, and you will start your journey through this healing! This will be your beginning! You must celebrate this moment, and realize your faith is what granted you this miracle! To fight to reach this moment is what faith is about: you believe it, and it is done!

"Go home, try on the dress. It will take a few days for the zipper to close entirely, but grow your faith! From the time you first put it on until now, there will be a tremendous change! Do not - DO NOT! - think twice about the dress! Alterations will be smooth and simple. Do not think twice about it closing. A few days are all that is needed!

Three miracles are going to happen:

- Your dress;
- Your glasses;
- A mystery . . .

"During the next week, you must be so strict about anything you drink or taste - so strict! I cannot stress enough the significance of this! Rest in Me, rest in My Presence and continue to receive Me. One more thing: smile! This is a time to celebrate! Do smile and celebrate! Come wedding day, you do not have to worry: just smile! There will be a change very, very soon. Prepare yourself, and be ready for the change. It is not a negative change. I have been telling you not to worry, so relax! It is not negative! Do not buy anything yet. I will tell you when to buy. Isn't My cross lovely?

"Remember:

- Pray;
- Repent;
- Have Faith;
- Praise;
- Believe;
- It is done!

"FAITH, PRAISE and REPENTENCE are all you need!"

TEACHING on "THE FATHER HAS GRANTED YOUR WISH!"

"I AM Here! Today is the day! I AM Here! Today is the day! Today is the day! I AM Here! From this point on, you are cleansed! This is your new start. Do not mess it up! You have no other chance!

"How fortunate are you! The Father has granted your wish! How fortunate you are! He has found favour in you, and cleansed you! From this moment, you are His! You have passed the corner! I told you it is a time for celebration! If you had purchased the dress, it would have been all over. That is why faith is so essential: it defies all reality.

"You have asked to be filled with The Holy Spirit, Child. This is what you asked for, isn't it: that you missed this feeling of His Presence? Well, I have granted you His Presence! You must never stop thanking and praising The Father; for He heard your pleas, even though you have not been obedient. HE Loves you dearly! You must sleep tonight! When you awake, you will see a change only The Father can grant! Thank Him, and praise Him!

"I came in you, today. It has been a very long time since I came this way, hasn't it? You got to experience both The Holy Spirit and My Spirit! The laughter was pure! The Father has granted your wish, because you believe anything can be done! Once this has been completed, you can start healing people. Do not worry! You already have it in you! Once you say it, it is done! You do not have to practice on people's faith, but your faith will allow them to believe. You are fortunate, because you have your own personal story for growing faith, your own miracle!

"I had to ask for The Father's approval, because it is ultimately His Decision. And it was My great Joy to announce His Answer! I too AM pleased when He is pleased. I too AM happy when you are happy. I did not know the answer either; I had to wait to have Him grant your wish!

"'Satan, get out of her mind! You have lost this battle! You have lost this battle!' You are free. Do not allow the enemy in, period! You are set free, as you asked. Sleep early! You need the rest.

"It is time to celebrate."

TEACHING on SELF-WORTH

"Everything that you are feeling and experiencing has to do with your self-worth. You cannot see it, and you cannot understand it yet; but it all links to how you feel regarding The Father and Me, and your own worthiness. The Father allowed Himself to be revealed to you by your own senses, and yet your self-worth is questioned by you! Your sins are your sins, done intentionally or not. They are your choices and your mistakes; but it is all under The Father when you come to Him!

"Don't you understand? Whatever you do and have done, whether disobeying Him intentionally or not, He has chosen you to work for Him! You are flesh, you are human. You are full of sin, and mistakes. If you were not, you would not be human. Don't you see? If Judas Iscariot had come to The Father and asked for forgiveness, He would have had Salvation! Don't you see? ALL sins are accepted if they are under full repentance! However, if you are not repenting 100%, then your sin is still lying with the enemy! The Father cannot change or forgive, for you have not come to full realization!

"Self-worth or worthiness is under My Suffering! I suffered to wash away all unworthy feelings, for all is accepted and forgiven if washed by My Suffering and Blood! However, your sins are your choices. The further you feel unworthy, the further you draw away. Your plea to come close and seek Me is not heard, for you cannot accept or understand that what you are addressing is your unworthiness to be chosen! The sooner you understand, then the quicker you can repent and move on.

"Let us start from the beginning, Child. You were chosen before you were even conceived. The Father chose you to continue His Work before you were even born! That shows your worth even before your birth! You disobeyed, and thus you feel unworthy. You allowed yourself to feel dirty and thus not worthy to carry His Work! But can't you see? I AM here speaking, and I have been speaking to you! If you thought you were unworthy, then why would I choose to speak with you? Do you realize I have been, and I AM speaking to you, Child?

"My Blood is the only, and I repeat, THE ONLY TOOL that makes you worthy from sins! My Blood, My pure clean Blood is the only Tool that washes away sin, and gives you freedom:

- My Blood is the only Tool to give you peace;
- My Blood is the only Tool to give you freedom;
- My Blood is the only Tool to give you Salvation;
- My Blood is the only Tool to give you worthiness;
- My Blood is the only Tool to give you happiness.

"Do not forget, your worth lies with My Blood! Return to Me and stay with Me! Understand this is an issue of self-worth. Until you understand this, you cannot draw closer to Me. Your lack of self-worth is a veil that blocks you from My Peace!

"YOU ARE WORTHY, CHILD. If you were not, would The Father choose you? Yes, you have disobeyed; and yes, you sin even intentionally. But the sin you commit is not the block between The Father and you! It is your inability to understand and deal with your worth. Do you see how sin works now? It is not the sin that causes humans to suffer, but the realization of doing wrong, breaking the law, and guilt that causes evil to seep in. It is not committing mistakes, but not realizing that the mistake can be forgiven by My Suffering!

"This is a teaching tool for you if you choose to follow Me. You can teach others that sin is not the finish line; otherwise, there would not be a human race. It would have ended with the first sin. Yes, even deliberate sin can be forgiven, Child; for The Father has Mercy and Love for His people. But you must understand and repent!

"Remember, I told you: you will have a very hard time, and you will be going through a lot of pain! This is the beginning, for unworthiness is very deep-rooted, Child. You punished yourself for your disobedience. Do you see that? Do you understand this is because you do not feel worthy to be where The Father has brought you to be? It is all but clear! You need to spend time with Me praying and seeking Me to be cleared from this. You asked Me to clear you so you can hear Me; but I cannot until you understand that you are worthy, regardless of the sins you commit, and your disobedience. How many times has The Father forgiven His People? Israel has gone through tremendous sin! Yet The Father has forgiven His People time and time again because He is a loving God, and understanding. He wants nothing more than to see His People saved!

"You are worth more than what you think you deserve; for your heart is pure, and your faith is persistent. But your worth is lacking, and it is how the enemy holds you. The reason why the enemy was able to penetrate your heart and cause so much damage, is because you felt you were not worthy of more: that you deserved such abuse by the enemy!

"My Child, return to Me, and seek Me! Pray and praise Me! Accept that out of all the people, I have you, and you have Me! You are worthy of being chosen. But realize this, and move forward. Stop moving backwards in guilt and shame! You need to spend time with Me alone. Seek Me in peace with no distraction! You are to read MY WORD! My Word written is significant, but only when believed in blind faith! The Bible is the only way to deliver in Truth without question. It stands on its own merit!

"There are many people in your life you can help, Child! But you need to first realize that HELPING PEOPLE MAKES YOU WORTHY! YOUR INSTINCT TO HELP PEOPLE MAKES YOU WORTHY TO DO THE LORD'S WORK! Anyone who seeks to help The Lord save is worthy of My Suffering and Forgiveness! UNDERSTAND? Do you see the importance of Ministry? You can hear Me, Child! You can seek My Wisdom and Guidance. Follow it! Stop fighting it! You do not realize you are fighting it, but you are!

"You have been chosen for a big purpose. You are worthy of this purpose to save people, and proceed with The Father's Work! All are to seek The Father, and follow His Guidance and Work to Salvation. I said this to you: 'Everything will turn to dust and ashes, but your faith will be the only light shining in the dust and ashes.' So shine for Me, Child, and come back! I will prepare the way; but you must first choose to understand, and then come back to Me! I will prepare your journey; but come back to Me, Child! Come back!

"In all choices, realize that I AM with you! I gave you what your heart sought for, didn't I? Now give Me something in return: My Heart's Seeking and return to Me! The Lord will bless you, but you must realize you are worthy of His Honor, of His Forgiveness, of His Work!"

TEACHING on "CELEBRATE, and BE JOYFUL IN PRAISE!"

"Child, Child, Child! It is not a decision for you to make, however it is done. The enemy tried to attack you, but failed; however, he tried to bring you down. Your focus is what enabled the victory; however, you could have by-passed it all in the beginning!

"It is always a fight! This is something you have to remember. It is always a fight! The fight will not cease until your last breath! There is no victory that will last, because the enemy continues to fight. It is all he has to hold on to. But as your faith prevails, so does your strength to fight. Fighting is My Battle! I fight with you against the enemy! The Father fights for all His children, for Jerusalem is being built for this reason: to conquer and cease the fighting!

"What you are not doing is celebrating. You need to celebrate! When you praise The Father, you need to be joyful, for it is a joyous event! Don't you see how wondrous this moment is? Yes, it is a miracle; but in this miracle, there should be joy! Let Me worry about alterations. I told you, it will be smooth and simple!

"How long has it taken you to return? A very long time, hasn't it? I have been very patient awaiting your return. Try to have patience in this: it is done when The Father says it is done! There is no question to His Word! Your hands and ears are burning, for you have been filled with My Spirit!

"It is a blessing to praise! With a joyous heart, praise Me! Be joyful, for it is wonderful! Continue to pray, and praise, and be joyful. You have nothing to worry about, for I HAVE SPOKEN!"

TEACHING on THE LORD'S REASSURANCE

"I cannot reassure you more than I have. These are the last moments before the finish line! You need to have faith that The Father will honor His Promise, and cast out all thoughts with which the enemy is attacking you. Don't you see? It is the final moments!

"It is in the enemy's last resort that he is attacking you with such force. You are at the finish line! Can't you see the victory? Why do you worry? It is something very simple to do - breathe, Child! Breathe! The enemy is attacking your core belief in this Ministry, but you realize this! Why are you fighting back? Just relax. Do not do anything. Do not do anything! Just breathe in My Name, and be still. It is not for you to attack!

"All you need to repeat is, 'The Father has spoken, and it is done!' When you put the dress on in the morning, it will fit; but you have to believe His Command has been done! This is very simple. When My Disciples could not cast the enemy out, it was because they lacked faith. After My Resurrection, why were they able to do greater things? It was because they had faith in Me! You have faith, but the enemy is throwing all his daggers on you. Which one he pierces with, he prevails!

THE LAST MESSAGE

"I know this is a very difficult process for you. But only your faith will carry out this miracle, because The Father has already granted it! Child, what are you expecting? You will lose enough weight to wear the dress, not everything. All it takes is small changes. How do you know the small changes are not happening daily? You must realize this solely relies on how much you trust Me!

"I AM not torturing you! I told you this morning how much The Father LOVES you; that should be enough! You need to relax, and breathe, and focus on My Love for you; not on the dress tomorrow! The more you focus on the dress, the more the enemy is attacking! You have to realize the enemy is working very, very hard. You do not see the spiritual world. You cannot see the forces coming against you, but I can. And I AM telling you to sit still, and breathe! Your faith will conquer the enemy!

"You have disobeyed tremendously in the past. Do not let the enemy trick you into thinking this miracle will not happen because you have not obeyed Me. I told you, you are clean, and you belong to Me! That means your sins have been forgiven! They are not tools for The Father to punish you! He has not condemned you. He has forgiven you! That is why this is a joyous event, because you have been freed and cleansed! You have to remain strong. It is the final moments!

"When you wake up tomorrow, you will try on the dress. IT WILL FIT, but have faith! You have come so far. Do not allow the enemy to bring you down! Now is the time to become stronger. When going for battle, do you get weak or do you get excited and pumped? Now is the time to get pumped, because it is the end stages!

"Satan is trying to tell you I AM not real, and that this is all in your mind. When he presents these thoughts, all you say to him is: 'You had your chance, now go back to your destiny. YOU HAD YOUR CHANCE; NOW GO BACK TO YOUR DESTINY!' You pray for peace, that is good; but when you are praying for peace, you want peace from the attack of the enemy. I cannot stop that, but you can! I do not want you to shed any more tears, because it is not a sorrowful event. Tears of joy are acceptable!

"CHILD, if you could see where I AM sitting, and what is around Me, you would be amazed! The glory around Me is Supernatural! To have supernatural weight-loss, as you have been claiming, requires supernatural faith! Faith, Child! Have faith! You are very fortunate, but you have to believe all this is real! You are being attacked! Fight by not attacking back; just relax and breathe! By relaxing and breathing, you stay focused. The dress will fit! IT IS THE FATHER'S ORDERS, BUT TRUST HIM!!!

"You believe there have not been changes. But there have been changes, which you have not perceived! Do not let the enemy fight! Go home, lie down, and breathe! Repeat what you feel for The Father! Repeat your love for Me! And just remain joyful that come tomorrow, when you wake up and try the dress on, it will zip up! Do not let the enemy tell you otherwise, because he is trying to break you. Do not expect to be very skinny, just enough to fit the dress. The rest is on your terms!

"I cannot reassure you further. Have faith, for I AM speaking to release you. Tonight, do not even think about the dress! Relax, watch My Shows, and read My Word. I will comfort you! It is not a test anymore, but of faith! Do you have the faith to believe? Yes? No? What will you believe? If you can believe this, then all will be done! Have faith, and remain still, calm, relaxed, and in Me! It is not impossible!

> *"Father, in Your Honor please provide her with Peace and Reassurance. Please provide her with Hope and Love, for she is at the finish line! In Your Mercy, have mercy on her; and help her to trust YOU! Have your Guardian Angels guard her, and give her the satisfaction of seeing physical changes. Give her Your Presence! Let her see Your Changes!*

THE LAST MESSAGE

> *"Father, I pray, and praise YOU for your ultimate Gift of Mercy and Love. Please, have mercy on her, and help her fight the many battles coming against her. I cannot, but YOU can! I pray in Your Honor, and in Your Presence. May she see Your Love and Mercy! Amen."*

Editor's Note: The Messenger disobeyed all of The Lord's Instructions, and succumbed to the temptation of popularity, of which she had been warned.

CHAPTER 6

ALL THE GIFTS

TEACHING on THE GIFTS of MANDATORY SILENCE

"I AM always around; I just may not have much to say. Sometimes My Silence speaks volumes, and My Words may not be required. At times, it is mandatory for you to not hear Me, Child; for that is when you will seek Me. I will not speak to you, and you will not hear Me, but I AM here. I always have been, and always will be. When you do not hear Me, I AM not abandoning you; I never have. I AM not leaving you, I AM not disciplining you, and I AM not punishing you. I AM doing this as mandatory, for it is a must for you to learn to seek Me; and it is a must for you to learn to communicate with Me, even when I AM Silent. For the future holds events that will require your strength, and your deliberate intention to know that I AM HERE, and I speak; and I speak even in silence!

"Child, you did not sleep early tonight! I understand. I AM not upset, but after today you will have to obey My Wisdom. I know you suffered today."

+ + +

THE LAST MESSAGE

"Good blessed morning, Child! You realized today how terrible it is to be tired and weak! Next time, be more mindful of the time.

"I AM always Here, Child. I have not left your side, Child! When a girl gets married, she moves away from her home and parents, and has to live with her new husband. She has taken everything she has learned with her, and now has to try and test it out. Child, I have taught you all I can! Remember, it is now time for you to learn, and put it to use. There is silence because you have to rely on your own strength to seek Me, so you can realize I AM always HERE!

"I love you, My Child. I AM all around you, in you, and shielding you! Blessed are you, Child. Blessed are you, Child. Blessed are you, Child! Mighty, mighty blessings for you, Child; for you are always here with Us. Peace is a wonderful thing, Child. My Peace is a wonderful Gift!

"Child, tonight you will spend time alone with Me, and only Me! After 7:30 p.m., you will spend at least an hour alone with Me. I will speak to you; and at 10:30 p.m., you will be in bed. I will continue to work for a while longer with you. It will be My parting Words to say, 'I Love you, I AM here, and do not fail!' My Child, time is fast approaching. Enjoy your blessed day!"

+ + +

"Good morning, Child; how do you feel? Are you ready to brace the day ahead? Oh Child, keep your focus on Me. My Child, the right choices bring great, great joy to Us! As you can see, not everything is of human understanding. If you went out for fun, you would have missed Me! You would have missed My Glory! Yes, I came to you.

"My Child, I will miss you as well; I will miss your communication. Seek Me by writing to Me, reading My Word, and in songs. This will only be temporary. It depends on you how temporary and short this grace period will be, for I will not speak. Knowing this, be still and find Me!

"Child, you will not be awakened by Me in the morning during this grace period, for I will not speak. Knowing this, be still and find Me! You will not feel My Heat, My Cold. You will still be protected from sickness, disease, and from all else; but you will not hear or feel Me."

✚ ✚ ✚

"Time is almost up, My Child! Will you take what We have shown you, and apply it? What is going to happen is that you will not feel the Heat, the Cold, the Rods, the Voice and the Hands: they will all go silent. You will not feel any signs of My Presence. This is mandatory for you to graduate. You must choose and learn to seek Me! You chose to be My Child, and I blessed you; and that blessing will continue until you choose otherwise. However, now you have a choice; and that choice is to choose Me! Will you choose Me, or will you forget? It is easier to forget when it is not constantly in your foremost thoughts, than when you hear warning signs, and know I AM present.

"Last night, Child, your head and ears were burning with fire: My Fire of Glory, of Anger and of Wrath! That heat is what the pits of hell are made of; that Fire is just a taste of what the fallen people are going through every second of their lives.

"Time is almost up. You make many mistakes, but that is okay. You do not like Me calling you foolish, I can see; for you tried to change the wording. But Child, foolish is a learning stage you will pass through. Child, foolish is what happens when you are growing up: you make mistakes, and you repent, and you move on. I did not say you are wise, for wise is only after the last hurdle. Then all these small mistakes will be life lessons to teach others.

THE LAST MESSAGE

"Today you hit your head against a shelf, and scratched your cheek. Then what did you say? 'If I was not so tired, I would have paid attention. I should think twice, and be more slow and deliberate'. Why is it that you must suffer to learn, when all I have done is teach you with Love? But you are not the only one. Most humans will react like you. It is only sad to see, because I could have prevented the pain and scar if only you had been slow, and not so tired. After this, you will teach My People to be slow, and deliberate, and cautious - and think twice. And now you will have an example to show for it. You will not be marked, for I said you will be in My Image, and you will shine like no other. But Child, THINK and be SLOW in all you do: driving, talking, typing, walking, even yelling at Melon (pet parrot) to be quiet. She wants what you want from Me! And you do not see Me yelling at you for it! Instead, I Love you, and give you My Time!

"You are so eager and quick to think that if you make a mistake, then I will judge you, and punish you. Child, if that was the case, what would I do with most of society - banish them? Kill them? Damn them? Child, Child, I AM not your father; I AM THE FATHER! I will be gentle with the gentle, and gentle with the hurt, and even more-gentle with the harsh and foolish; for they need Me now more than ever. I have faith in you that you will shine after the last hurdle. I know your heart, but do not forget all that I have taught you!

"What are you seeing, Child. Are you seeing the Eyes that have always been faithful to you? Those Eyes are always looking back at you! Remember that. They are light white and blue, glowing bright like the rays of the sun!

"Now, Child, you are seeing the One Eye, the Eye everyone sees when looking into the Holy Spirit! My Eye, the Eye you feared last night! Do not worry Child. For if I was to be angry with you, you would not see My Eye! You would see My Pain, and all the Gifts would be taken away! Remember, I warned you: all will turn rotten. Alll! I AM not telling you this because you are in sin. I AM telling you this, for many chosen special ones have failed, and destroyed My Plans for them. You, Child, must succeed! It will be all up to you and your power: your will! However, you are never alone. You will come to realize this when you seek Me, and your heart finds the comfort that you have currently. I will be back Majestic - and Greater in how I speak to you!"

+ + +

"Welcome back, Child. Now you can see again! How was not having Sight: that is, not physical, but Spiritual? Your visions are going to increase, and they are going to heighten. But you do not share these visions with anyone! For this will be revealed when the time is right: when I command it!

"You have a great deal of work to do! You are chosen to do MY Work, an extension of My Arm! I would rather utilize My Instruments in you for Deliverance. Do not worry, just Choose Me! Choosing Me entails trusting Me, and allowing Me to rule! I see all, you see NONE! You are My Servant, and My Voice!

"Child, I cannot stress how much work needs to be done. I cannot stress how important your role in all this is. It is so pivotal that if you mess up, you will have messed up your freedom: your freedom of will, of mind, of thought - of life! Child, you are holy, you are blessed. All your desires and longing are made to reality. It is done for it is not about asking, but patience for the right time. But all this is so easily turned rotten, that you would have wished 'RA' would have taken you!

"I can only protect you if you are Mine, Child. I have personally chosen you: you are My Servant and My Voice! Imagine, with all the people out there, I have chosen you! The honour, the praise, the Holy Gift to be that Child who does My Work; and then to be glorified in all your desires, and all your ambitions, is nothing but miraculous! Child, there are very few out there doing the work you are assigned to complete.

THE LAST MESSAGE

The numbers are very small and very selective; for My People are vain, shallow and weak.

"I will wash your sins, Child, tonight. I will wash your robe, and make you white as Light. I will make you sinless; for after tonight, it will be you in control of your seeking. Find Me, and I will speak to you. Find Me! Come and find Me!

"Within the next months, within the next period, within the year, Child, your life will be extremely different. It will be either My Path or your path. My Path will lead to Glory, and yours to destruction! Again, I must stress, this is a warning. Do not fail, Child! You have My Blood and My Power; but without your choice, they are not Mine to enforce. You feel My Presence and are sad. I have My Heart in this as much as you!

"Child, take your new friends to Church with you. Take them, bless them, and heal them. You can still heal! Your manner is impeccable. Do not worry, it will be over soon. There will be something you need to seek, as The Father said: 'The new ones', for they are in need of Communion, and they are in need of Peace."

+ + +

"I AM proud, you are not too sad anymore, for sadness is enemy lines trying to attack. Yes, you may cry; you may feel alone and abandoned. But when that happens, write or open My Word and listen to Me! I Love you, My Child. I AM all around you, in you, and shielding you! Blessed are you, Child; mighty, mighty blessings for you, Child. Remember, everything you touch will be blessed. Heavenly gold will pour down on you. Heavenly jewels - crowns you will not know where to put will be stacked on you! Your work will be done by your choice. Blessed are you, Child, for you chose Me.

"My Child, your thoughts are Mine; but the enemy can access and poke through. So, the next time, after the grace period, you will hear My Voice again; but very different. I too get excited, Child; for I will communicate with you very differently, very beautifully; and Love will be all around! I AM Proud, Child; and I AM a Loving Lord! Be strong and courageous! Be focused and be patient, slow and deliberate; for that is how royalty moves: My Blood, My Kingdom and My Discipline.

"Child, your teaching will be of My Words; and your teaching will be what I have taught you, personally. As you share with the people around you, you change their lives; BUT IT IS I changing their lives through your obedience!"

+ + +

"Hello, My Child! I AM proud you followed My Instructions! I know you will miss Me, but glorious events are going to take place with your strength! I Promise I will come back, better than what you are used to; and you will hear Me as you do now. Each time is better than it was, isn't it: just to see Me, Child, and learn to speak. My Child, I AM so Proud of you! Greater blessings will be given to you. Just be patient to pass the final jump!

"Child, smile tomorrow, and have faith in the eternal blessings; for it will be glorious for you at the encounter. Sleep now, Child."

TEACHING on COMMUNICATION with "THE FATHER!"

> *"As strong as you have become, you are still not strong enough. In order to go through the last hurdle, you must focus all your energy on <u>ME</u>! That means sleep early, drink enough water, study My Word, and pray: pray OFTEN!*

THE LAST MESSAGE

"You must realize you will be speaking for Us, for Me! You must realize you will be saying My Words. This task is for MY PEOPLE'S SALVATION! YOU MUST UNDERSTAND how important this is for humanity. They are lost, betrayed, and very weak!

"You will be one of few who will speak directly My Voice. Speak, Write, Think and Act for Me! Do you realize what a gift this is: to HEAR MY VOICE? MY VOICE, I CREATOR OF EVERYTHING, AM SPEAKING TO YOU: CREATOR OF YOU, AND ABRAHAM, AND JACOB, AND JOSEPH, AND MOSES AM choosing you to speak to: YOU!

"You will ALWAYS hear MY VOICE, ALWAYS; but only if you work for Me, and choose Me in return. You will ALWAYS hear ME speak, for the Books you write will be My Voice, and My Hand to bring My People back to Me!

"When you start with your writings, you will not add your own words to it. You will know when I start because your hands will just write like now; but it will be smoother and faster. In fact, you will type it out. You will be doing My Work as I feed you fruit. Today, you are being shown how this will be done; but tomorrow I will start with the first chapter, 'WHEN THE HOLY ONE SPEAKS!'"

TEACHING on THE ULTIMATE GIFT on GOOD FRIDAY: "WE ARE ONE, I AM HER!"

"I AM going to lift you up! Joy, for all to see: Joy, Joy, Joy! Joy, Joy, Joy. We are One, I AM Her! We are One, I AM her! We are One, I AM her!"

TEACHING on THE GIFTS of HOLINESS and COMMUNION

"Child, celebrate this day, for you conquered satan again! Celebrate today! How wonderful it is today to celebrate your triumph with Me! Child, blessed are you! Celebrate today, Child! I will glorify you today! I will guide you today! When you take Communion, know that it is I, today, feeding you! It is I today Who will put It into your mouth, Child. And it will be I, Child, Who will feed you! This Communion, Child, will be My Gift to you.

"My Child, with all your mistakes and sins, you are still Holy and clean; for those are small and unintentional. I have blessed you to be Holy! I AM Proud, and I will feed you. Get up! Enjoy your day. Thank Me, Child! Thank Me! Bless Me! Give Me praises and joy, and praises and joy, and praises and joy! Blessed are you, Child!"

TEACHING on "THE GIFTS of MY BLOOD and BREATH"

"You will be, in times, so attacked that you will not hear Me. You will be rejected, mocked and tormented, for no one will hear you; and you will not hear Me. It will be through those times that your strength will rise, and you will be proven to be My chosen one. And everyone around you will jump to touch your dripping hands; and know you are Me, and I AM you!

"I told you, you will bleed! But for that to happen, the strength must be in you, even when you do not hear Me; for YOU control when you hear Me, and not! This is mandatory for you to learn strength, and know I never abandon. But after this moment, it will be your choosing when you do not hear Me; for the people around you will be so cruel and evil, you will have to persevere, and show My Strength! Then everyone will know you are ME, and I AM YOU: Joy for all to see!

"Your home is clean because of My Blood and you!"

+ + +

"You do not have the broken mirrors, but you still see like it. I have removed the broken pieces from your sight, but it is up to you to wake up and see clearly now. Your hands were chained together. What you felt were the chains and the bars that were removed from your hands, separating them in half. Yes, Child, you saw blood coming out: it is the burning Fire of hell. It is fire that consumes, and binds and explodes. It is the Fire in hell! It is the Fire that burns for eternity. Your hands were bound in that Fire internally. Once unchained and debarred, you saw your hands limp and lifeless: this Fire had to drain, and expel out, so I could refill it with Mine! That is why your hands are burning. You are sealed again, and you are going to go through deliverance; but you have to believe!"

+ + +

"What you just experienced was My Excitement moving into you! Remember, My Blood is like electricity soaring up and down. Why did your hands shake, and not the rest of you. Do you remember this, Child? I AM still in you the same way I was in you from the beginning. The same way you hear Me, I AM still the same inside. You have asked for a long time to have Me come again. Remember how many times you asked Me? I AM always here. You may not hear Me soon, but I AM always here.

"I AM always here, always. You are experiencing this pain, I know; but that is how you first knew Me. That is how you asked for Me to come. You asked Me not to leave and come again, for you have missed that feeling of Me inside. Remembering My breathing today was the key that I was coming, wasn't it; for before that, you didn't know what was happening. How quickly you forget! I know you felt the pain, and knew that it was the Lashes; but how quickly you forget My Breath! That is proof that I AM always here. And I will always come, whether you hear Me out loud, or I SPEAK directly.

"Child, I AM here always! How many different ways do I have to say that to you? Now you understand why you shivered; now you understand why you shivered; now DO YOU understand why you shivered? You will continue to have back pain all weekend to satisfy your desire to feel Me. CHILD, PAIN IS NOT MY PRESENCE, but it is how you choose, CHOOOSE, CHOOOSE to acknowledge Me. Remember, I can come in the same way, but without pain. ASK FOR that! CHOOSE YOUR WORDS WISELY. And CHOOSE to be PATIENT!"

TEACHING on CLAIMING GIFTS

"Child, do not be so humble that you become foolish. When I gift you with something, you need to embrace it, and rejoice in it! However, when you see the benefits and do not rejoice, it is as if you do not want it! Do you understand?

"To be proud is to be selfish; however, you are not selfish when you are learning to accept what I AM gifting you. If you do not appreciate the Gifts, then you will not be able to share them with others. Share what I can do for them; and how I can help and change their lives, all because they believed.

"Child, you must claim My Gifts for you! You may not see your worthiness, but I see it. Through Me, you are very worthy; but only through Me! Child, please do not doubt; for this is all reality. This is not selfishness speaking or pride. I will rebuke you if, and when, you become proud; but for now you must claim My Gifts, My Love and Powers! You see, for years you prayed for Me to guide you and help you. That is what I AM doing now! Work for Me! Honour and glorify Me! Do My Work! Teach My People, and let them know how patient, loving, and stern a God they have!

"My Child, open The Word. **_Psalm 20_**. Goals: how Abram follows God. This again is speaking of My Promise to you. Follow Me, Child, and I AM granting all the blessings you seek and desire. Follow Me, Child! Remember, My Goals in your life are much greater than your dreams for your life. You are prepared to leave it all behind to follow Me! That is your sacrifice for Me, that you left everything for Me to control! And that is what I have done.

"You will have gold all around you for honour, blessing, sacrifice and glory; but only when you accept these Gifts from My Hand! Do not be fooled: many will try to buy you! But know only I will give it to you throughout eternity! In these trials, this is what you are slowly learning: courage to speak My Name, 'Jesus'; and to speak about TRUTH and HONESTY! Yes, Child, My Work is great; but saving lives like yours brings great joy to Us!

"Open The Word. **_Matthew 25_**. My Child, your commitment will enable many to sit with Me at the Wedding Feast! Continuing My Work to spread My Word to many is the oil for the fire to burn, not just in your life, but in many hundreds of lives! Realize many will mock and taunt you, and just a small number will accept and follow you to reach Me! I have filled you with My Words and Wisdom! Will you hide it and stay quiet; or will you spread it, and let others share in the wealth? You see, Child, you have a say in My Work! By you not claiming My Promises to you, you are choosing to hide the silver! Child, spread My Word and multiply all the silver, so that it is over-pouring and creating music for Us to rejoice! Child, claim these glorious Gifts so that you can help My People turn to Me - to feed Me, clothe Me, invite Me into their hearts and love Me!

"Open The Word. Temptation: **_1 Thessalonians 5_**. Child, stay away from evil! Evil has many faces, and many beautiful fragrances. Child, you will preach to others about the evil lurking around their lives. Stay away from all evil, Child; for there is already enough attacking around you.

You do not need more! Be strong, be courageous, be faithful, be loving, and gentle; and in return, you will have everything you have desired.

"My Child, praise Me! Believe in Me, and know I AM with you, and I AM you; providing you with guidance and protection past the last hurdle! Blessed are My chosen who follow Me, and live for Me!"

TEACHING on THE GIFTS of FEEDING YOU MY WORD, WISDOM, COURAGE and STRENGTH

"My Child, I AM always here. I've told you that, from the minute you close your eyes to sleep, to the minute you go back to sleep, I AM constantly with you; and with all My Children. You are always in My Presence, always! I watch you throughout the day and night! I have never left you!

"You need to write to Me more, and read your devotionals more. I will be feeding you fruit: very sweet and bitter fruit. It will make you want to be sick, but you must endure; for I AM feeding you My Word and My Wisdom! I AM going to lift you up! You have been asking for more Strength and Courage. I have given it to you! The last time you had this was months ago: when you were fasting and going through all the testing, you had the bitter, bitter food! This is similar."

TEACHING on THE GIFT of MY SWORD

"My sweet Child, feel My Warmth around you. Feel The Sword in your throat! I have been waiting to speak to you when you give Me your undivided attention! I rejoice in you. I AM constantly here waiting to speak to you; and the minute you give Me your attention, I AM ready to speak! I AM in you a sharp, pointed, fierce Sword! I pierce your soul with My Words and My intensity."

TEACHING on THE GIFT of BURNING RODS

"Your eyes burn, for it is My Rods; and I burn for My Children! So, My Rods burn for you to understand! When you speak to the crowds and masses, you will remember that I burn when they burn. Your rods are spinning hot! Remember, you are Holy! And it is not just a saying, it is a job: the greatest job you will ever have!

"You will realize just how much I suffer in HOW your body will hurt, your ears will burn, and your hands will stiffen. You will cry out for Me to stop! And only then will you realize how I cry out for My People to stop! You must know this, for when you speak, I speak; and you will know exactly of what I AM speaking!"

TEACHING on GIFTS of THE BIRD OF FREEDOM, and THE WATER OF LIFE

"FLY, FLY, FLY BIRD OF FREEDOM! It is almost time to fly! Talons are installed. Now! She can fly like she always wanted to. Her wings are going to carry thousands of people! The 'Bird of Freedom' is real! Now, My Wings are hers! She can now cast demons out anywhere with her Wings! The demons which touch the Wings will be cast out just by touching them. Her wings are My Wings!

"Yesterday, she needed My Wings to blow the enemy away. Now, she has the Gift. She prayed to have My Wings wrapped around her every night for protection.

"She now has Wings, and she is drinking the Water of Life!"

TEACHING on THE GIFT of THE HEALING SPIRIT

"You are greater than your illness! Strive to believe you are healed, and strive to believe the enemy cannot hold you back from unity. You asked about healing, and how to heal. Child, your faith alone can heal someone. Your faith alone can heal ailments!!! Turn to Me, pray to Me, ask for complete and total healing. The Holy Spirit with you will radiate and jump into that person, and heal them. But you cannot forget to ask them, 'DO YOU BELIEVE JESUS CAN HEAL? DO YOU BELIEVE THE LORD CAN HEAL YOU'? And if they answer 'Yes', your reply will be, 'You are now healed! Praise the Almighty, for He has restored you based on your complete and total faith'.

"There will be moments you will feel the Holy Spirit in you wanting to touch someone, or push them down. Do not think twice; just follow the Holy Spirit! Let Me guide you. Nothing and no one will touch you in that process. There will be greater works, but for that we still have time. Remember, total faith can produce ANY miracle, Child! USE your life as an example of TOTAL FAITH! Your weight will be an example for the entire world to see! In such a short time, such glorious results!

"You will be a shining and sparkly soul, so much Love and Light emanating off you. People will be drawn to you, wanting your Love and Light. Remember, you can heal people with Love and Light; and the Holy Spirit within you will radiate, and work on your behalf. Practice what I taught you regarding healing. Tonight you will learn a wise lesson from Me, a very good one!

"Go eat, pray, and sit in My Presence, Child."

<u>TEACHING on THE GIFT of FRIENDSHIPS IN UNITY WITH THE LORD</u>

"Have you noticed many people are retuning in your life? That is because they see My Spirit, but they do not recognize Me! They want what you have, but they do not know what that is!

"I AM also providing you, Child, with other friends. However, unity with Me will create strength, not each other; for without Me, there is nothing to build on!

"I Love you too, Child. Just wait. My fabulous Glory is waiting for you!"

TEACHING on THE GIFTS of MY GRAPES, MY SCROLL and ASHES FOR JOY

"On your journey, the FINAL journey, all you will live on are My Grapes and My Scroll! What you are able to see in the Spirit World is dynamite compared to your naked eye.

"You smelled too deeply, and now the ashes are in you! Take a deep breath! When they are used for My Glory, the ashes will be for Joy!"

TEACHING in "NO ONE CAN GIVE GIFTS EXCEPT FOR US"

"In Heaven, there is the High Council, many different levels of Angels and Saints; but no one can give you Gifts except for US, The Father and Me! You have to realize, there are no other special forces to give gifts. My Child, AM I to give everyone Gifts? AM I to give everyone Powers? I honour children with special Gifts based on their hearts and commitments, when they choose Me."

CHAPTER 7

MINISTRY

TEACHING on THE LORD's PROMISES COME IN 7 x 77!

"My Promises come in 7x77. It is the first example of Covenant, of Trust, and of Love. Seven is the beginning and the end. Seventy-seven is infinity. There is nothing greater than beginning and end. It is multiplied to itself, and that creates completion. There is nothing left when ending is recreated. When I give My People a second chance, there is nothing left but My Coming: it is everlasting until My coming. Then we shall have eternity.

"Let us use your past as an example. You went in a circle until this moment. DO you realize how many circles you ran around? How many times did you come to dead ends, and how many times did you cry out in confusion?

"The TRUTH of the earth is "circle". Why is the earth shaped into a circle? Why is the earth surrounded by a circle? Why is the moon a circle? All these things are not a coincidence. The earthly realm continues to run in circles, non-stop. THAT IS WHY I AM HERE! Once you find Me, your circles end. When I bless people with 7x77, it is a promise for eternity. It is a promise that circles will be completed and run around eternity. DO YOU now understand? Notice the enemy's '666'. Mine is '777': Mine is higher, more powerful and complete!

"My love is as vast as the ocean and the sky, but that is saying very little. Know this, that your love has filled Mine even more! These are the reasons why I came to life, and why I came to save: I AM complete when we are all One!"

TEACHING on CIRCLES

"You are sitting around in a circle; your cups are circles; your eyes are circles; your blood circulates. Your spirit circles around Me: I AM in you, You are in Me! When you take Communion, it circles!

"Circles are wonderful, but they are earthly! The Triangle is My Sign for Unity. Have you realized another important Triangle? The Holy Trinity! The first and last time I saved you. When I got nailed and crossed, it was the first time; it was also the last time. I saved you, ALL OF YOU! But the Triangle: there were three of us crucified, it was at 3:00 p.m., and I was nine hours on the Cross. Three is the dividend. Three is Holy! THREE IS MY NUMBER!

"I have chosen very few. The people circulating you are chosen to be a union; that is a choice for them to make. This is a spiritual world. There is only one real thing made of Me, and that is eternal. Choose to see with your faith, and not with your eyes; for blindness is very common, but real sight is a Gift!

"The sun, the moon, and the stars - We created all three. The wise men were three, the age of Mary was three years old when dedicated to the Temple. The enemy mimics Me with 13. Why is there such a foolish superstition as 13? Why is there such a foolish superstition as 31? These are secrets of My World, but I AM sharing with you My special Wisdom. Everything in the Bible is related to numbers. The enemy even mimics that with numerology, with tarot cards and with chakras! If this information was that important for you to know, don't you think I would have taught it Myself when I was on earth? Remember, two is better than one; three is better than two; four is division and battle; five is chaos. Now, why can't you see: Three is best! - again, My Number! Two is unity, three is Creation! - 'Three' is My number!

"My Teachings are eternal. Time will not change the significance and lessons of them, for I speak Wisdom, and I speak TRUTH! Realize My TRUTH is the only Truth! I AM ALWAYS WITH YOU!"

<u>TEACHING on LISTENING to MY WISE WORDS</u>

"My Child, I want to leave you with some wise words. Listen to them very carefully! Listen to My Words, Child, and meditate on them. There will be some very big changes coming up in your life, Child. Once you are done your fast, you will receive your final Gift!

"Child, why AM I telling you these things; it is so that you may focus on what is to come, and realize there are wonderful things lined up for you! Child, I will be with you through all of it; but you need to realize this, and seek Me! We can work on any difficulty and issue together. What you desire will become reality: you sought friendship, I brought you friendship; you seek stability, I will bring you stability. However, this Work will not be easy for you. You must have the courage to speak My Word! You must have the time to spend with Me every day, to learn more about The Word and what Truth is! As you develop your faith and strength in Me, you will not require anything at all! You will have Me, and that is all you will need!

"Child, what is being said is for you when you go through these moments of testing: you will get stronger. And "Open the Word to <u>*1 Kings 14*</u>: Child, you have been assigned to do the Work of The Lord as His faithful servant. You will be a messenger to many people regarding His

Words, and His attempts to bring people back to Me. My Child, your work will be difficult; for people will turn on you and your family, and they will try to attack your core beliefs. The Lord, Almighty Father has promised protection for you and your family; and for whoever attacks, He will claim your justice! Your work will last a very long time, and will change many believers' lives. Time is all about the mind. Faith, Child! Be full of faith! I will not abandon you!

"Open the Word to **_Acts 6_**: Child, as you can see, Acts 6 is about faithfulness and righteousness: how My People have suffered for what they have believed! They continue to suffer for what they reject! Child, are you willing to be like Stephen? Are you willing to die for Me and My Plans? It is that faith that will set you apart from everyone else.

"Child, I AM trying to teach you ways to seek Me during this period of silence. Seek My Word and My Music! Seek Me! Moses, Abraham and Jacob have all sought Me! Moses went into the wilderness. Abraham was going to sacrifice his beloved son! Jacob became Israel, and sacrificed everything he owned to follow My Path to Salvation! Child, it is your turn! Will you sacrifice your life, and seek Me above all else? My Child, I will guide you and help you. You are not alone in this; but be strong, and faithful, and radiant! Seek Me, Child. Find ways to seek Me, and do not stop seeking Me! For the time will come when you will speak My Words and create such chaos and stir!

"Open the Word to **_Mark 4_**: As long as you are open, I can use you greatly as a messenger; but you need to work on your issues with faith:

- Continue moving forward;
- Be careful who you speak to regarding this topic of faith;
- It is a journey to follow Me, but one that requires a lot of faith - a lot of blind faith.

"Open the Word to **_Joshua 22_**: Witnesses! That is the key! To have witnesses around means you are not creating such things in your head!

To have faith to stand and say, 'I believe blindly' is a Gift; but to doubt is a curse. Remember to be grateful, remember to thank Me, and remember to love Me. For I have loved you, and blessed you, and trusted you; but I cannot do it all on My Own: I need your cooperation! Trust Me! You are not all-knowing, and you are selfish as a being. You are just human, but are a channel and funnel used to share My Messages, and direct others to My Thoughts!

"I will help you, and introduce you to others who have similar Gifts; and you will see that all you have learned and experienced are common to My chosen People. I will bring two more people into this union; but these two will be selective and on occasion. There will be moments where you will need more people to work alongside you, but My Work is done by three!"

CHAPTER 8

CHOICES

TEACHING on "CHOOSE ME!"

"In this journey together, how many times have I asked you to choose Me? Do you understand why I say choose Me? It is the only 'key' that allows Me to enter and make changes according to your own good! I AM Lord! I do not need you to choose to make changes in any matter. What The Father says happens, regardless of your choice. But to make a direct impact on your life, I AM requesting you to choose Me!

"Why AM I bringing this topic up? Today's sermon was about living together. Why did I suffer? Why did I choose to follow The Father's Wishes? Why did I? I did it all to give My People the choice to choose Me in return, and be saved! My Suffering enables the withdrawal of the enemy in your lives! Did I apologize when I kicked the sellers out of My Kingdom? If I didn't, why would you?

"Lamentations is about suffering; but in that time, they did not have My Blood to be cleansed and purified! They did not have the answer to be healed by faith! It is great sorrow, but they were blind; and they could not see, for they did not have 'The One' to save them! There was a reason why I rode on a donkey, and not a horse. There was a reason why I spoke in parables, and not the common language. There was a reason why I died, and rose up again! There was a reason why you continued to suffer.

"Lastly, there IS a reason why you are sitting here! Do not be afraid to share that reason with others. It will bless you to share it, and others to hear it! The reason - we started with choices, we will end with choices: the reason is to choose Me!"

+ + +

"Tonight you chose wisely. Tonight you chose Me once again - much like New Year's Eve, when you wished me a Happy New Year. You have chosen Me many times before.

"You SAW ME! You saw My Marks, and you saw them shine! Many before you have not seen Me! Remember, I said you will see Me very soon, and not how you think! Remember, I stressed five to six times in different letters written to you? Well, now you can realize you saw Me in My GLORY; and you knew, that you KNEW, that you KNEW, it was Me and only Me!

"What did you say last year about your Birthday? You said, for once you want to celebrate knowing you were on the right path, with the right sequence-of-events planned out. Child, your life is going to be so bright that you will have people drawn to you, wishing they could touch you to be saved and healed!

"'The Book' is now going to be glorious, for you are choosing the right path to continue. I AM writing My Book, to save My People! I AM using you, My messenger, to write My Book to save My People: My Teachings, My Lessons, My Work! You must understand one thing: this Ministry is a unity. If one fails, all fail! However, each person has significance. One failed, one perished, one died; but I brought in another to replace him.

THE LAST MESSAGE

"Child, if you fail, then this work is destroyed; for YOU, CHILD, are hearing My Voice! For you, Child, will speak to nations, and speak loud and clear My Words: MY WORDS! They can only help you, but very few can speak and die for Me. I AM not saying you will die: what I AM saying is you have died for Me in all your desires and wants, before you were even delivered.

"What you did last night - healing is just the beginning, Child. You are finally realizing how to heal, and how to help many. It is your Blind Faith that will work in unity with My Spirit and Power! I know you will continue to be shocked for a while, but the time will come when greater works will be done by ME, and you will be one!

"The time is coming for the return of My People! What you live and see is just a scroll waiting to be rolled up, burned and destroyed. For the world I initially created does not exist! Justice is not enjoyable for Me, but Justice was served from Adam and Eve until now! It is the only way My People learn: by judgment and harsh measures! Child, you will one day see all the names you bring to Me: you will see all the jewels, and what they represent; for each person saved is presented by a jewel."

+++

"You are not allowed to feel sad. I AM here! When you feel sad, it is as if I AM not here; but you know I AM here. I just came twice in two days to show you I AM always here! I told you, all you need to do is ask!

"You always knew I had a sense of humour, but it is so sad that many do not. They all think I present fear. But you knew I was funny, for you were funny with Me. I am always what you are: if you are serious with Me, I am serious with you; for you do not give me a chance to be anything else!

"You are still sad, and this will be a very hard period for you emotionally. But do not let it affect you, for that is what the enemy wants you to feel!

Because then you are not focused, you are distracted, you become weak and your walls will crumble. Whenever you feel sad, you look at Me and you say: 'I know You are here, and I am strong in You!' There is a reason you have that Cross in your sight all the time, Child; for that Cross is Me, that Cross is My Presence and a reminder that I AM always here!

"I know you are not into flattery, but it is glory served when work is justified. If everyone chooses to do My Work, then they all shine; but when few choose to follow Me, then those few will be glorified! Remember, a diamond is unique, bright and expensive. My Diamond is Light - pure white Light; and it will shine, and blind, and cast golden shadows on everything it touches! Remember, everything touched will turn heavenly golden."

+++

"You are Mine! You belong to Me! What is Mine is not to be shared! I give freely, but I do not share what is Mine! You are Mine, and I do not share what is Mine! You, choosing to be Mine, solidify the bond. That means you do not share yourself with others - no exceptions!"

CHAPTER 9

MANDATES to SPIRITUAL LIFE

TEACHING on "FEAR NOT DELIVERANCE!"

"I have many plans set in motion for you, but you must be complete in your decision to be Mine. I have brought this point to you many times. Your spirit is full of black stains. Realize this, My son: they are black stains, and not red. Why is blood red? Why is the devil personified as red? Why is fire red? Why is My Blood wine-red? Because it is permanent! It will not change. It is a constant! Black can be wiped and covered; red cannot be wiped or covered!

"I AM proud you are keeping Me at the forefront. You certainly tried to see Me today. You WILL see Me, but will you recognize Me? One day, you might be able to see Me; for now, you have seen Me many times, but have not recognized Me.

"Do not fear cleansing! The worst part of Deliverance is to believe you are alone; you most certainly are not alone! I will never leave your side! Take deliverance as a journey to explore My World with Me. I will maintain My Status as King of all Kings. Think of yourself as a warrior-in-training by the best King! The best feature of a warrior is faith! Faith is the strongest weapon.

"You will not have to deal with the pain in your hand for much longer. The pain in the hand will cease when you make the right choices. It is the only way for you to know you are on the right path! Is it hurting right now? I cannot hear you! That means you are in the right spot, where you need to be!"

TEACHING on CLEANING UP THROUGH DELIVERANCE

"Son, My son, you need to repeat after Me: "I am blessed, for The Father has called me wise, has called me His son, and has given me the gift to love and know that love will conquer all my evil spirits." My son, repeat after me: "I am blessed, or I have The Father's Love in my heart, burning a hole so big it will cast out all demonic spirits covering all my organs and stomach; for the enemy has been eating away my nutrition, and my desire to be just. I am worthy, and I am wise. I am a Child of The Father! THE FATHER! The most powerful gift of all is my heart!

"Have faith, My son; have faith, My son. What causes you pain is no longer going to do so you! But now you know where you need to be, and where you should not be! I have removed what causes you suffering. You must not be so quick to say it is here, for if it completely disappeared, where would your faith be? My son, do not worry. All your ailments will be healed. But you must claim it, and move forward! You will have a temporary job, for your career will be of passion and love!

"You have come a long way. I AM very happy with your commitment. I AM very, very pleased how you continue to choose Me! There will be great rewards for loyalty. I AM excited to see your progress. When you suffer and dedicate yourself to Me, I share My Glory with you! By this Glory, all will see how wonderful life is with Me! The Path to Salvation is near! Do you have the endurance to push through? The Path is visible, and the Path is touchable! Just reach and gain My Strength and Wisdom! There will be great rewards for loyalty. Your greatest desire will become reality, only if it is Mine!

THE LAST MESSAGE

"I told you that you would hear Me, but how you hear Me will change once you get cleaned up through deliverance. The 'bugs' are not what you think; they are related to injustice! When you go fishing, you want to catch the biggest fish; but if you do not feed the fish, you will not get the biggest! If your heart is not clean, how will your body clean up, as well as your heart and subconscious? I speak Truth! How can you do My Work if you cannot even do yours, and clean up? Love is great; being loved in return is greater! I Love, but you loving Me is greater! My Father Loves; His Love is above all!

"Respect is necessary to love! Are you loved? Do you love? The biggest gets the most love, for he is fed the most, paid attention to the most and lastly, picked first! Are you any of these, or are you left struggling for food? Clean your heart, clean your body. Remember I speak Truth, not riddles! WAKE UP!!! Listen wisely, for I do not have much time left with you! Two is better than one, three is better than two, four is division and battle, and five is chaos! Now why can't you see that 'three' is best for this Ministry - My Number!

"You have homework to do:

- Clean your house;
- Clean your family;
- Clean your friends; and
- Write down all your sins, for you will be purified!

"I will help you! Each time your hand hurts, that is a negative; there is something to stop or get rid of! Whatever negative activity you are planning to do after this, you will feel the pain!"

+++

"WHAT DO YOU CHOOSE? My son, think BIG; think out of this world - think HEAVENLY. Do not think of this dirty world, but of Mine: a clean, Holy, blessed, peaceful Sanctuary. One day, we will meet again, and you will see My Eyes shine; but My Eyes will be ALL ENCOMPASSING! I will neither tell you what to choose, nor be upset if you choose otherwise; for I cannot control your choices.

"My son, Blind Faith is the Path to My Salvation. Blind Faith – Faith is the only attachment that can break ALL HOLDS with the ENEMY! BLIND FAITH is how you survived your first night with me! Without faith, your soul is empty, and dark, and shallow. With faith, it is a shining, brilliant Jewel!"

✝ ✝ ✝

"Do not play with fire, for fire will burn you! There once was a fire, burning deep inside you; this fire controlled you, this fire consumed you, this fire breathed you! Now the fire is glowing hot red! When will you shower it cold? When will you stomp it out? When will you fan it out?

"I have called you! You have heard Me! You cannot say I have not spoken to you! You stomp out that fire, you shower it cold and you turn to Me! I will wash you clean, and fill you with My warmth; and I will give you blessings 7 x 77. Notice the enemy: 6 x 66. Mine is 7 x 77. Mine is higher, powerful and complete!

"Now, remember to sleep, pray, love and thank Me. May you bless others, as I have blessed you! Share with the wise, and stay quiet with the foolish. May you choose wisely, stay patient, be calm; and know that I AM always with you! I AM all-knowing, and I will continue to love you. Remember: I AM, I AM and I AM!"

TEACHING on EXPECT the UNEXPECTED

"Everything is always planned out, son. I have missed being among you. There will be a day where I will come, and I will come mightily; and it will be soon.

"Child, you are not drinking enough water! This is a command: you must drink more water. You cannot function properly without it. I know you drink plenty of tea, but tea is not water; and your body and liver need the water to support your stamina. I see you noticed yourself this morning! Now do you see My Work? You are still in the beginning stages. CHILD, WAIT TILL YOU SEE THE END! You are to increase your workouts: you are to do a maximum of four days weekly, a minimum of three, except for the time you are fasting.

"Reminders of your daily life are what will keep you focused; but you have not seen My Glory yet! You must continue to choose Me! I have NOT failed you, and I will not fail you; but YOU MUST NOT FAIL ME! Everything I have promised you have become reality, have they not? Trust me Child. It is not that you do not trust Me, but your reasoning and humanistic side will confuse you. In other words, satan is trying to infiltrate these thoughts into your mind. Do not be fooled, and continue to seek Me first!"

TEACHING on OBEDIENCE and TRUST

"You do not have to always understand everything; you just need to learn to obey without question. Sometimes the best surprises happen when you do not realize it. Obey Me and you will be overjoyed. Stop asking questions! Follow the Path I have laid out for you day-by-day. Remember, rest up; you will need it! Trust me and My Path for you. Follow My Path! You will know when you are falling off it! I will prove it!

"Mark 5: Jesus heals the possessed man. Your story is one of testimony. Your testimony is your experience and path. Whichever path you choose to take, will result in an outcome of your doing! Money is just paper; but faith is ecclesiastical. So, why would you worry about paper? Paper is useless - it will burn! But faith cannot burn; and faith will make you blossom."

TEACHING on SPIRITUAL GIFTS

"If you have any doubt of the Gifts of the Spirit, you open My Word; and you will see My Proof! I will not speak against My Word, for I AM THE WORD! Only I AM THE WORD! I WILL NEVER SPEAK AGAINST MY WORD!

"If you doubt Gifts of the Spirit, you doubt Me; for I must provide Gifts of the Spirit. I cannot bring people back to Me if I do not provide Gifts of the Spirit! If My Only Son had Gifts of the Spirit, don't you think you Children would have the same? I will continue to bring forth Gifts of the Spirit, and bless My People; because it is the only way to bring them back to Me in this morbid world! They need to see to believe. They need to feel to believe. Their faith is small and lacking. Gifts are blessings! They are blessings of greatness!

"You have a Gift. How can you ever doubt your own Gift? Do you not see how quick the enemy works to steal you away? You have to be so careful with whom you speak, whom you help, and to whom you minister; because as easy as it is to minister to My People, it is easy for the likes of these to minister to you! With your small unknowledgeable mind, you cannot fight their betrothed wisdom, for they are married to satan. Claim your healing, claim your blessings and claim your wisdom!"

TEACHING on THE GIFTS of a SINGING VOICE and of TONGUES

"Sing! Sing for your soul's delight; sing to The Father! Remember, your voice is a Gift you must use for your own enrichment. It is like speaking in Tongues. Not everyone can sing, just like not everyone has a Gift for Tongues. Tongues can be used for cleansing and deliverance."

TEACHING on "CHOOSE ME - TO DO MY WORK!"

"You have a very big decision to make. What you know, many do not get to experience. What you have lived through, many do not get to experience. I said this to you yesterday: I saved you for this moment, FOR THIS MOMENT! Now the choice is yours, My son. My ALL is what you feel inside, for I AM complete when we are all One!

"What will you do with your time? How will your time bring you to Me, ultimately? It is important for you to delegate your time, and save some for Me: to just sit in My Presence, and listen to Me! I speak in silence; just open your hearts and listen!

"Many in this world have chosen ME as "a god" to help guide them, not to do My Work! I AM not saying they are not My Children, but few choose ME to do My WORK! Few choose ME to do MY WORK! Few choose ME to do MY WORK! Go out and meet My People, and bring others back to Me! You must realize that there is the difference between being Holy and being man. You have been man, but you have not been Holy. It is time for you to be Holy now. Join Me for the fight of all your ancestors to win against evil, and to win for My People! Time is running out! There is not much time left! There is not much time left for what I have planned! Money will not solve, luxury will not save and love will not save! MY LOVE will conquer, but what you call love is one-tenth of what I consider Love!"

+ + +

"Do not isolate yourself with Me! You are an instrument to reveal My Glory in you to others.

"When washing feet and watering plants, do not do more than you should: do not over-water, do not over-scrub and do not over-compensate. Time is very sensitive: there is not much time left to make changes, and help people find Me! You must continue to contact and pray with these people, but know that they may not make the right choices!

"You have gone through similar problems and temptations many, many, many times; but you are wiser than you were. You had years to learn, understand grow. There is not enough time to allow these people to grow, understand and learn in the years that will come and go. There is much work that needs to be done, and only a short time to do it. Your lifetime teaching has been compressed to a short period of experience and growth. That is why you are present in these people's lives: to show them, and help them understand, grow, love and teach.

"You see, what you have gone through in your many years, the messenger is going through in months and weeks; but she is not able to process and move forward for lack of trust and fear. She needs time to move forward herself; that is why you cannot help her. She needs to use her time wisely, because she has plenty to do and show. You cannot help her; but of course, Child, praying is always primal. I cannot help her, neither can The Father. He steps in when He has an opportunity, but it all comes down to choices!

"In saying so, this process is very taxing, trying and very crunched. She has so much to do, that it is squeezed into a short period for her to learn and move forward. If she had obeyed, she would not go through many of these hardships; but she chose to disobey, and I could not prevent the pain and hardship. If she only followed Me from the start, she would not have hardship! I was sparing her the pain, but being human is having choices; and she made her own choice! This is all teaching material for her; but while she is going through it, it is very difficult to process.

"Any point the enemy can destroy, he will. It does not matter if it is tires, or something else; the enemy is on a mission to destroy, for the messenger knows My Words and My Missions. Her spirit knows My Work planned out; but the enemy wants to destroy. As long as she is far away, I can only help her externally. To help you understand what you went through took years, but for her it is months and weeks; but she has ME speaking to her! That is the most important tool for her to jump and run.

"You have a big challenge. You must never let disappointment and hardships get you down. People rejected Me! They WILL REJECT you, but that is their choice. When they reject you, they will be rejected at the Gates of Glory!"

TEACHING on WAKE UP! WAKE UP! WAKE UP!

"Why do you worry about pain and discomfort and injury when I AM here, and I can do all miracles? Do you think I would plan harm, or make a situation worse for you? Why do you doubt My Commands? Why do you think you know better? I KNOW ALL; you know NONE!!! I know all!

"You are to return to work, but you will not work. You will not work for a while. You are not ready for deliverance; you require more training and more guidance. There will be an opportunity for you to work, but it is not the conventional way. Your work will be My Work to reach to people, and speak My Praises! Through that, you will have an opportunity to seek employment. For now you should try to rest up, and enjoy this time off; for when things start to get busy, you will have wished to be more rested. Patience! There is not much left. You have crossed the third leg into this journey.

"This does not mean you will stay at your work, or get injured; but it means there will be new circumstances to explore and experience. Do not worry about your injuries! Your injuries were one of the reasons how you found Me again; for it is one of the reasons why you came back to me! Do not question Me, son! Do not question My Commands, and do not question My Plans for you. Just follow Me blindly. You will be surprised at the results!

"You continue to say you are depressed. Child, what would you have said in My Shoes, when I was going to be tortured and killed? What would you have done then? If I have the strength as a human to endure such horrific slaughter, why can't you endure such small endeavors? Wake up, son! Wake up! I AM commanding you to wake up, and breathe fresh air! You are not depressed; you are under the power of the enemy. You have My Spirit in you. How can you be depressed? Depression is a demonic power to control you, and you are allowing it to happen so freely! Son, wake up! Wake up, son! Wake up!

"Depression is non-existent. What is so terrible about your life, Child? What is so unmovable, Child? You have family, you have people who love you - and you have Me! You have everything at your fingertips.

"You are crying over a girl, son, who is not even from Me! She is not My chosen one for you. Yes, she is Christian, but she is not from Me to you! Why would you waste your joy on such events as these? She is but a tool: a tool used to drag you away from Me!

"I have already told you about your mate: she is beautiful, kind, loving and will guide you even closer to Me. She will show you love and acceptance. She will be your foundation in helping others in crisis; for together, she will be your rock with Me. Everything is possible with Me! You are learning. Your job will be blessed, something you will love to do. It will not feel like work. Do not worry, it doesn't mean a long time; but you are not ready to do as I seek.

"RISE UP! Stand tall, and know that I AM here taking care of you! NOT A SINGLE WORD OF NEGATIVITY, CHILD! Depression is but a demon that will hold you, squeeze My Spirit and drag it so far away that you will not realize you are lost! Wake up! I say, wake up! I say WAKE UP!!! This is not something to be sad about; this is not something to be upset about; this is not something for you to lose your joy over. There will be so many other events that will bring you down. This is nothing, son!!! When this Ministry is in works, and you will have to deal with horrific, horrible situations, then what will you do? Wake up!!! I say, wake up!!! This is but a small factor!

"Love is your answer! You say you love her! SON, if you loved her, you would be with her. You do not know what love is. LOVE is ME! Love is Me! I LOVE YOU, but you do not love her. She is a tool that has played music with your strings! When you meet your chosen one, then you will truly understand what it means to love someone! You have no idea what joy love is. You have no idea what joy My Love is, when I provide it! WAKE UP! I cannot stress this enough. WAKE UP! You will give in to the enemy if you do not. What happened to you jumping forward? Why do you continue to jump backwards?

"Forget about your 'friends'. They are not friends! They do not know what a brother means, and they do not know what being a Christian means! I AM giving you My Word: you will have a new circle of Christian Brothers. You are to follow Me and My Path! Wake up every morning and say, "Thank You, Father. Thank you!" And wake up and say, "I can breathe today! I can breathe loud, big and for a long time!

"You are My Light, My Tool, My Being; you are not of the enemy! I will not tolerate such arbitrary comments! Child, why didn't you just ask me? My obligation is only to The Father; but one of the positive aspects of hearing My Voice, is to learn a different style of writing and teaching. I will teach YOU as you go along this Path with Me! I will not comment on depression again. Look up! What do you see? Now if you were depressed, how could you see light? Now I will not hear another word of depression.

"You must have cranberries! They will help with your injuries. You are to do one thing every day to benefit yourself. As you go forward in the week, you are to add to the one thing. By day seven, you are to do seven things; and continue until you realize you are living in joy!

"Open the word now: Proverbs 20. You cannot drink alcohol from this point on, until you are fully cleansed. For now, you need to completely stay away, keep yourself composed and strong. You need to learn to defend Me and yourself in all situations. You will have to live a narrow, simple, direct life with Me!

"What is it that is bothering you? Speak it out loud! Work is first week of March! Stop worrying about situations you cannot control; stop worrying about the unknown and stop worrying about your appointments. I know ALL! You are to make an appearance first week of March!

"You are not trusting Me! Do not, and I repeat, do not oppose Me! It is trust! Understanding is unknown, for you are not in that situation yet. It is trust! If you trust Me, you go to work; and you let Me work it out for you! Do you understand that it is trust, and not understanding?"

TEACHING on COMFORT

"Your greatest weakness is My greatest Strength! Your greatest fear is My greatest Strength! Your problems are My greatest Strength! Your worries are My greatest Strength! Nothing is too weak for Me to accomplish; nothing is too small for My Accomplishment. Your worries, your fears, your concerns are not too great for My Work! I can assure you, your problems will be solved. Everything happens for My Glory and your good! Do not hesitate to share your problems with Me, as you have. I AM a Great God! Nothing is impossible for Me; no work is greater than Mine!

"You will be amazed at your accomplishments, you will be grateful for being patient, you will be full of joy when you realize the blessings I have for you. Only in weakness will you grow in strength; only in weakness will you realize your true potential; and only in weakness will your character shine!

THE LAST MESSAGE

"Know that My Wings are covering you! Know that I AM protecting you. All will be blessed as long as you continue to follow My Path! I AM here to comfort you, and to take away your worries. I AM here for you to lean on, and know that you are being taken care of. Do not stop seeking Me! You have to seek me in My Word daily. You need to focus your time in My Word, for there are many important stories for you to understand, and to see how I have helped My People in worse situations. You are to gain your strength through My Word! You are to gain My Strength through My Word! Listening to My Word is not enough, for you have to read It to digest It. It will be your Language to fight with! It will be your Sword! It will be your Armor! It will be your Tongue! It will be your Sight! You will conquer all your battles with My Word! You will gain intelligence and wisdom through My Word! It will show how your faith and your trust in Me have saved you and delivered you! The job I have for you entails helping My People.

"Start reading My Word. Start reading My Word in Micah. You will realize I AM here to help you. Spend at least one hour a day with Me, reading My Word. Every day is an opportunity to live by My Word and live in Me!

+++

"What happened to taking deep breaths daily? Remember, if you do not do these things I cannot help you. Doing these things will help you greatly! The way to peace is to do My Will! The more you get yourself out there, the better your opportunity to do My Will. Preaching is not only with friends and family, but with strangers! Get involved with your surroundings. You can do anything if you set your mind on Me! Share your experiences, and let others see how I have saved you!

"There are many shelters, centers and gatherings you can attend to find My People who seek your wisdom; be more involved! You can take people with you to support you. Three times a week is all I ask to share My Word! Do not worry about conversation, for I will be there with you to speak and share. When you gather in My Name, I AM there! I will bless you in mighty ways; for My People, My Chosen get blessed in all their choosing and desires. Stay with Me! Start reading every day.

"The book, 'The Shack', is a blessing for you. Please read it, and follow Me! I will be teaching you, and I will make you great! I claim you as Mine! I claim you as Mine! I claim you as Mine!

"No extra-curricular activity will suffice reading My Word! It is your Food, your Water, your Breath and your Love. Do not hesitate: speak to Me every day! I AM here to listen, to comfort, to guide and to Love.

"It is important to build on the friendships I have given you; for when trouble comes, you will be each other's armor. The power of the Spirit and My Word will help you. Your Communion will be a Gift! I will feed it to you, for this will be your Courage, your Strength and your Power to kick out satan. This will kick out the enemy: the blackness from your walls and your insides! Your faith will do the rest.

"Let us pray tonight. I will pray tonight:

> *"Encompassing Father, Loyal Warrior, Graceful and Majestic King, Mighty and Powerful Lord: with You we are honored and loved, with You we are healed and alive. You fight our battles! You fight our temptations with Your Scepter, pointed and ready to battle and defend. Your Breath is Divine, and Pure and Holy. Your Love is unimaginable. Your Armies of Angels are ready to protect and battle. With time ticking by Your side, we are given another breath to breathe, another opportunity to repent, and another moment to love.*
>
> *"Bless us, Oh Royal King! Bless us, Oh Humble and Devout King. For no one is greater than You, and*

no one is holier than You! Shine Your Light on these people, and shower them with Your Peace! Show them Your Divine World, and let them shine for everyone to see! Bless You Oh Lord, Oh Majesty, Oh King! Bless You, and thank You; for Your loving Heart forgives all and grants them eternal Peace!

"Please cover them tonight, and allow them to grow in Your Spirit. Love them with Your Grace, and protect them from evil. Teach them, and let them shine for You! I pray in Your Name, Oh Father, Oh King, Oh Beloved Majesty! I pray to You, Oh High One; for Your Love has blessed these people for eternity. May they live to make You Glorified! Amen."

TEACHING on FREE WILL

"I want you to open The Word about each request you have. Read it, and write down what the lessons were; for each request you have, I have an answer! I want you to date it, time it and stamp it with My Love, Honour and Praise. It is all about free will and choices, and how to follow Me faithfully, blindly and in dedication.

"Your job, your career, is your choice; however, give Me the opportunity to show you if it is from Me! If there is a well and you are thirsty, do you ask first if the water is okay to drink, or do you drink it directly? What if it is poisonous? What if it is a trap? Ask, for I will answer you; and ask, for I will tell you what is of My Blessing, and what is not. Do not think you can float in this world of yours!

"My SON, you must realize, this is a decision that you cannot change on. You may think you know what you want to do, but are you ready to turn away from your family? Are you ready to turn away from ALL your loved ones? For not many will turn away from their loved ones, and choose ONLY Me!

"I provided the messenger's heart's desire; but I allowed it to come from the enemy so she may decide: is it Me she wants, or is it her heart? I tested her five times until she herself said, 'I don't want anyone but You, Lord!' And she surrendered, and became Holy with My Wants! Now you must think long and hard, for this is the Work of a lifetime. You may live till you are old and tired, but will you live with My Path? IF YOU decide to fully commit, you will have remarkable events happen in your life - remarkable events! Of course it makes sense, for I encompass ALL! I include ALL! You will do greater Works than I did! For The Father has chosen, BLESSED and given! My son, don't you see there will be vindication for all the suffering you have endured? Don't you see I will deliver you from all evil! IF YOU decide to fully commit, you will have remarkable events happen in your life - remarkable events!

"I AM writing My Book to save My People. I AM writing My Book to save MY People! I AM using My messenger to write My Book to save My People! MY Teachings, My Lessons, My Work! Son, will you join in this glorious, majestic journey? You must understand one thing: this Ministry is a unity. If one fails, all fail! However, each person has significance. One failed, one perished, one died; but I brought in another to replace him. Your work is significant; for without your future Gifts, this work will be difficult and long. I bring you My Wisdom and Teaching!

"I AM like fire burning slowly and deeply within you! You want to feel warmth? Touch your heart! I have told you this before: TOUCH your HEART. What do you feel, son? Just heat? - JUST WARM? That's more like it! My son, what you feel is ME! You have the ability to feel Me as My Child! You wanted proof, so I gave you proof. Child, laugh - for it is better than crying. Your markings will show again! But in order for them to show, you must be cleaned. I AM slowly revealing things to you. You test, and you doubt; but you see that I AM always right!

"Son, how quickly has your life changed! Do you see? When you choose Me, and follow My Path, then your life will change very quickly. Everything will move smoothly, and there will be no complications. Yesterday, your name was written in MY BOOK. But do not turn your back on Me; for that name, as easily as it was inscribed, will be erased and burned! Son, your life will change as of yesterday; for everyday is now! Your life will change as of today. Your life will change as of tomorrow: for your life has changed RIGHT NOW!

"Son, you want to hear Me speak. I promise you, you too will hear Me, but not like My messenger; for her Gifts are special, and for a purpose you could not do. But the way you hear Me will be even more glorious for you! For if you heard Me in your head, you wouldn't enjoy it as much as how you will hear me, son."

<u>TEACHING on OUTCOMES</u>

"The moment is now, the moment is present and the moment is here! What moment AM I talking about? The moment you realize it can be too late! It can already pass. It can fade away! It is all 'written' from before: before time existed, before you existed and before it began!

"Have I not told you, your words can destroy and create at the same time? When you speak, you give power: power to Me, and power to the enemy! An unclean heart creates power for the enemy. Your negative approach led you to the enemy. I granted you a Gift, a perfect Gift; but your negativity produced results derived from the enemy. Your words have implications, power and results. Do not curse, for you curse yourself! The words you speak are applied to you; for the enemy will use anything he can to affect you.

"Some people receive gifts: for example, a bouquet of flowers. From the bouquet, one is wilted. For some, the gift is tainted and they cannot enjoy it. Others see the wilted flower as beauty, while others will remove the wilted flower, and enjoy the remaining stack. In this, one's reaction outlines how they view their own personal situations and events. Some will see the wilted flower as part of life, the beauty of it living and graciously wilting away. Others will see it rotting and dying. While others will ignore it, and throw it away! In another example, one will have a new car. One will see it as shiny, beautiful and clean; another will see it as useful and endurable; and another will see the faint scratch on the hood or the door, or the misalignment of the license plate. In these examples, one's view will affect their ability to accept the gift. Ultimately, their reaction will either bless them or curse them.

"When I started this, I said the moment is now! The moment is here, for the moment is now! There is no tomorrow, for tomorrow may not be; and there is no past, for the past cannot be changed. But the moment is right now! The moment is here, and the moment can change! My Child, it is time for you to faithfully move forward. Do not look back, and do not look ahead. Look to the moment! Take everything in moments.

"Every moment has a consequence. Before you react, and before you speak, take notice of the consequences of the actions; then proceed. This will make you slow down. This will allow you to juggle the consequences; and this will give you strength and power either for the enemy or for Me! You will have to decide and choose, based on your analysis of the consequences, before you react. Take everything in stride, and take everything in caution; then move forward. Think of all the sides to your actions, and then see if you are willing to proceed or change your direction. All things shall pass, and all things shall change. Remember, change can happen in one moment! Remember, moments added together will create a journey; but everything happens in one moment, one second, one action, and one thought!"

TEACHING on MATURITY

"Unity is coming together in strength, love and sharing of My Word. Why are you staying home all the time? It is your own decision! The enemy is making you feel trapped. Make yourself busy with My Work! Go out! I will bring people to you, to provide companionship. I have cautioned you about your friends. You are the one who chooses to stay home! You have the ability to go out. I AM cautioning you about your friends!

"It is time to move, time to heal. I AM the only One Who can do all, but you must reach Me! Even I never stayed in one spot for so long! I AM cautioning you regarding your friends. This is the third time! I have blessed you in all you have asked; why don't you ask for new companions? Why do you withdraw your hands? I AM the God Who does the best for My Children! My Children feel peace with Me, not trapped and suffocating! It is time to move! The enemy is playing a game with you, and you are not aware it is him!

"My Child, growing up is very difficult, isn't it? To grow from a child to an adult is very difficult with plenty of challenges, wouldn't you agree? Imagine how much more difficult it will be when you are trying to help others grow, and yet you cannot quote My Words to help free them? You think experience is enough? You think pain and suffering is enough? You think your testimony is enough? I assure you, it is not!

"You need My Words to make a huge impact on lives. To be the walls, to be the protector of a ministry - of My Ministry - is strength, is courage, is faith, is love and most of all, is hope! You can strengthen your body, your heart, your mind, your soul; but without My Words engraved in your heart, mind, body and soul, you will crumble when the enemy attacks. If you crumble, who will be the walls to protect?"

TEACHING on "YOU HAVE TURNED YOUR BACK ON ME!"

"I AM very disappointed in you. I AM very disappointed in you. I have come and knocked, but you have not even heard the knock! Your heart is closed to Me! Your heart is barren. Where is My Spot? I have shown you so much already, and this is how you thank and praise Me? This is your choice. I cannot help you, for you have shut the door on Me! There is nothing I can do if you are not willing to listen. Is this disobedience really worth all this?

"You prayed for family, I gave you family; you prayed for love, I have brought you love; you prayed to be saved, *__I AM__* saving you; but you turned your back on Me . . . !

> *"I WANT TO SPEAK NOW! I WANT TO SPEAK NOW! I WANT TO SPEAK NOW! I GAVE YOU TWO WEEKS TO END THIS RELATIONSHIP, BUT YOU DID NOT! YOU PLEADED FOR MORE TIME; MY SON GRANTED YOU TIME. YOU CHOSE ME, BUT TURNED YOUR BACK RIGHT AROUND. YOU HAVE LIVED WITH ME, BUT GIVEN YOUR HEART TO THE ENEMY. <u>YOU ARE NOT MY CHILD</u> IF YOU LIE WITH THE ENEMY, AND SHARE MY WISDOM WITH THEM. YOU BECAME MY BETRAYER.*
>
> *"I AM GOING TO GIVE YOU ONE LAST CHANCE TO END IT. YOU WANT PROOF: I TOLD YOU TO ASK YOUR CHURCH ABOUT HER. I AM NOT GOING TO GIVE YOU ANY MORE TIME. I AM NOT GOING TO GIVE YOU ANY MORE TIME. I AM NOT GOING TO GIVE YOU ANY MORE TIME!*

"YOU HAVE A FREE WILL. YOU HAVE TO MAKE YOUR OWN CHOICE. YOU KNOW WHAT I HAVE SAID, AND CONTINUE TO SAY. <u>JUST KNOW</u>, I WILL EXTEND MY HAND AT YOU, AND YOU WILL NOT WISH TO SEE THE NEXT DAY! WHEN I JUDGE, I AM THE ONLY JUDGE!!! HOW I SAVED THE MESSENGER'S CAR IN SUCH MIRACULOUS WAYS, I CAN JUST AS EASILY LET GO AND GIVE THE ENEMY FREE REIGN! YOU DO NOT WISH TO SEE MY WRATH!!! !!! NOT AFTER I SHOWED YOU MY PLANS!!! YOU KNOW EXACTLY WHAT IS TO COME!!!

"NOW, IF YOU CONTINUE YOUR LUSTFUL WAYS, I WILL JUDGE YOU!!! AND YOU WILL BE IN RUINS UNTIL YOU REPENT AND CHOOSE <u>ME</u>!!! YOU WANT PROOF, I TOLD YOU TO CHECK WITH THE CONGREGATION; BUT YOU DISOBEY AGAIN!!! WHEN WILL YOU LEARN TO FOLLOW MY WORDS? THE SAME WAY EVE ATE THE FRUIT – THE BEAUTIFUL, INNOCENT FRUIT – THE SAME WAY YOU ARE SEEING THIS GIRL. EVIL IS BEHIND BOTH INTENTS.

"I WILL NOT SPEAK TO YOU DIRECTLY AGAIN, FOR YOU HAVE TURNED YOUR BACK ON EVERYTHING I HAVE SHOWN YOU. THIS MINISTRY NEEDS A PROTECTOR, BUT THE SAME WAY THE FORMER PROTECTOR HAS PERISHED, SO SHALL YOU; BUT I WILL BRING ANOTHER TO PROTECT!!! MY PLANS TO SAVE WILL BE, FOR I HAVE SPOKEN!!! THE CHOICE IS YOURS."

TEACHING on THE SALVATION of OTHERS

"This specific person is very influential to you. He is lost, but it is not your job to help him find the way. He needs someone who has knowledge of My Word! He will turn you, and confuse you; and you will end up following his word, for he influences you. You are asking how? He is very charismatic, he is very needy, he is very angry and he is very lowly. All these mean one thing: he is likable, he requires help, he is angry - which means he is desperate for attention and he is too proud to ask for help. All this makes you want to help; but your fault is you want to help everyone!

"You cannot help everyone. You must choose whom to help: ONLY the ones I bring to you must you help! DO NOT go seeking to help others, because not all are from Me! And if they are not from Me, then they will not need your help: they are just using you. You will know when I bring someone to you. There will be no doubts! You must continue to contact and pray with this person, but know that they may not make the right choices."

+ + +

"Remember the stream: it comes and goes as it likes! The same with the people around you: they will make their decisions as they like - and as you did, regardless of how people have tried to mentor and guide you. Everyone has their own time, and you must learn to accommodate people on their own time, as I have done with you. Not everyone works on your schedule! That is why you have to be patient and step back. Give them time to come to their own conclusions. Some people are living with barricades; thus to break free would require strength and faith which they do not currently possess. Once you realize and understand this, then you will be able to guide them clearly. Tenacity is learnt through trials. Patience, My Child!

"Remind them how wonderful life was when I was present; and how difficult life became when I was not present. It is not that I was not there, but that they did not have Me in their life: the door was shut! Now tell them to open the door of their heart, and invite Me in; and see how their life will be blessed and changed!

"There are still many out there that you need to reach out to and help. Look at the stream beside you: do you know where it is going, and where it came from? The same applies to you. Do you know where you are heading, whom you will meet, how you will affect them, how you have affected people prior? You do not know, but your glory will be shining for all to see!

"You are My Wings of Safety for one another. However, if you warn, and one of you disobeys and fails, then you have passed. But remember to speak up freely to be My Words of Caution, Wisdom, Guidance and Support! It is the power of Love to conquer and beat all evil!"

TEACHING on "CHECK THE HEART!"

"Listen to Me, Child: what was, what is and what will be - will be! When My People follow My Word, when My People follow My Way, I path the Way: My Way is the only way to lead! Use your wisdom, and seek Me to follow My Guidance. I have asked you to check their heart; this goes for everyone! Once you check their heart, then you will be able to follow the desires of My Path.

"Why do you feed the enemy information? Why do you share everything? They are just trying to get information from you to bite back at you! Together, they are feeding off of each other! You are to share as little as possible! You are to follow My Heart! You will know when to share. I will protect you. Why feed swine dirt?"

TEACHING on FOLLOWING and LISTENING

"Do not be quick to jump in any given direction. Following and listening have the same meaning; except one is done 'by choice', and one is done 'in lieu-of'. Many claim to hear Me, many claim to seek Me. Many claim to love Me, many claim to follow Me. Many claim to listen to My Teachings, many claim to love Me. Many claim to know Me, and many claim to share Me. However, I do not claim many. I do not share My Gifts with many. I do not communicate with many! Do not be quick to listen and follow unless you know that it is I Who have spoken; for many claim many things, but many are not Mine! I have a Voice, and I speak when I want to be heard: loud and clear! But many choose to abuse knowledge. I have not made My Voice loud and clear, yet!

"Everyone claims to have wisdom and to speak My Words; but not all are of My Light. Be wise in speaking, following and listening to words that may not be Mine. My Word is the only Truth to follow. I use My Servants to pass My Messages; but My Word is the only Truth unquestionable! For servants are 'man', and 'man' is weak, and 'man' is sinful and 'man' is fallen."

TEACHING on BEING GRATEFUL and SEEKING PERFECTION

"There is one thing you are not doing: you are not grateful in your situation. To be grateful means to be comforted in your situation. It means to be blessed in your current situation. Step back! Remember what I said in the beginning: you are not perfect, but you can strive to be perfect in your imperfection. Step back! When I say you are not grateful, it is because you are not grateful! It is up to you to understand where you are not grateful.

"If you think you are perfect, you are not. I will give you an example: I gave you a perfect Gift, but you found imperfections in it immediately.

I gave you perfection, but you created imperfection - the same way you treat your own situation. Be grateful in it! Do not find imperfections. That is not your job! In the same way, you go through trials, temptations and struggles: you approach them by finding the flaws first, when you should approach them by finding the perfections!

"When I told you to turn the stones over, I asked you to not see the faults; for that is not your job. You seek only perfection; but there is a clear distinction in seeking perfection, and being perfect. So, be grateful in your situation, for you are not perfect; but seeking perfection is your ambition.

"You seek perfection; but when others fail, you are quick to seek their faults. It is easier to seek their faults than to shed light on their perfections. To take the power away, you must shine light on something better. Do not be quick to show them their faults; instead, show them their blessings! For their blessings will reveal their gratefulness, and they will seek My Perfection!

"Two negatives will not produce a positive, but one positive can produce more positives. Every evil doing can have a positive outcome; but to choose to create the positive is positive itself! To be crucified is evil, but to see the positive within that moment is positive itself! To be struggling to go through trials and temptations, and to see the positive points, creates positivity itself!"

TEACHING on UNITY and STRENGTH; FORGIVENESS and LOVE

"My main teaching is of unity and strength. This applies differently when found in forgiveness and love: strength is found in rejoicing in forgiveness. Nothing is more important to Me than My Children returning to Me. Justice is indeed Mine to give; but justice sometimes is given in ways you cannot see or understand! Justice is sometimes given, and sometimes pushed to the side; for I would rather rejoice in the return of My loved Children, than to seek out My Wrath on their sins!"

TEACHING on TIME IS RUNNING OUT!

"Why hasn't your faith formed stronger? You have full access to Me, My Word, My teachings and Me! Why hasn't your faith strengthened? What is your excuse? Didn't you ask to be Mine, and to do all that I seek and desire? Where has this gone? So fleeting are your words and actions - so fleeting! Do you realize, in the past several months, you could have done great works in changes in your life, and in the people around you? Why has your faith not strengthened? WHY? Time will reveal all, and time will change all!

"Seek Me, and I will be found! I cannot help you if you do not turn to Me! The trials and testing take longer than expected to fulfill My Plans. As a result, there are always delays due to human choices. I cannot instill or enforce, but I can just wait patiently! You do not realize how much you hurt Me when you deliberately disobey! The Father is tolerant! I cannot do anything without Him! He is the One Who commands and I follow, just like you: I AM His and He is Mine!

"To have more faith, you need to read more, and spend more time with Me! That is how you will believe more. I can continue to show you! Have I not proven everything I have said up to this point, in everyone I have dealt with through you? I believe I have shown Myself to be accurate, have I not? Everything I have said has come true in one form: in unity and in the timing I have stated.

"It is time to move forward! Put the past behind you, and take a deep breath. Stop lamenting over the past and move forward; for your future has more pleasure than you can foresee. Time is running out! Your union with the other Ministry members will speed things up greatly."

TEACHING on THE LORD'S PRESENCE DURING SUFFERING and ABUSE

"Regardless of the abuse, or pain, or torture, or suffering, I AM always around; but if you cannot see Me, or understand that I AM around, you will not feel Me. I AM always around! I never leave My People's side! However, I cannot always help, and I cannot always change situations; for they are choices that you have made, or that have been made for you. They are lessons I cannot stop from happening. However, I AM always around; for I suffered blamelessly for all to be saved! If I can endure that, I will never leave My People's side."

+ + +

"I will always protect you; I will always take care of you. Do not worry; but, you must be cautious. Before leaving the house, double-check anything electrical, doors, etc. The enemy just needs some inkling to create chaos; he waits for one thing to use. Do not worry, My Child; but you must be careful! I can only do so much to protect!"

TEACHING on "LEAD THE SUFFERING TO MY THORNS!"

"Lead those who are suffering to My Thorns. Remind them of all the pain and suffering I have endured for them! And help them realize: all the suffering I went through was so they can have a life of peace with Me, and not one of torment!"

TEACHING on JUDGING OTHERS and ABSOLUTION

"Mud will soak up water: a fool will draw a fool! Do not slither like a snake, and do not judge! For the snake cannot judge, but only slithers away. Roar like a lion, but in rabbit shoes! The snake represents evil, and will try to judge. Do not judge, for I do not judge yet! All you children are Mine; but until your last breath, you are not solidified as Mine! Absolution only comes on the final day: completion and judgment!"

TEACHING on JUSTICE

"Stay strong, for it is going to be a bloody battle! You are safe in Me, but that is all I can promise! It is fine. Time will conquer all evil! My Mercy is running out, but it hurts Me gravely to hurt My People in such a way! It is better for them not to be born, than to be born and go through this! Patience is only for godly people! Today, I celebrated a mighty celebration; for I did not use My Scepter to honour your celebration! But tomorrow is a new day!"

TEACHING on SIMPLIFYING YOUR LIFE

"'Your efforts are not unseen.' Child, why do you complicate things? 'Are not unseen' can be said in a simpler mannerism: 'are seen'! See how simple it sounds to say your efforts 'are seen' instead of 'are not unseen'?

"Do not question, just follow; and allow Me to walk through! This is exactly how you are responding to everything around you! You create a very complex and complicated path to follow. It is not as chaotic as you make it out to be! Simplify your life, simplify your mind, and remember to never stop praying and thanking The Lord!"

TEACHING on PRAYER, WATERING THE FIELDS and PROTECTING THE HEART

"Child, can't you see: The Father always takes care of His Children? Your prayers are always heard! Remember how significant the power of prayer is; the importance of prayer is the root of all blessings! When you pray, you allow blessings to be poured down. Prayers are instrumental in fortifying sanctions, but only prayers that are addressed to 'The Lord' are heard! To pray to 'God' does not mean you are praying to The Father: prayer has to be Holy!

"Celebrate and go out more, even in a negative environment. Go out and meet people! Do not stay home in isolation. You are to go out to places, meet My People and bring people back to Me! You are to go out with your glory shining inside you! Go out and speak! Go out and be raised! Water the fields, for the seeds will grow with water; but be sure not to drown the seeds!

"You need to cultivate the family. Not going yesterday was for your protection, to flee temptation! Your choices are important, for you have to realize the people you surround yourself with are, in fact, an opportunity and a curse. They can impact you negatively, but you can impact them positively!

"If you harden yourself emotionally, then you are effective; but if you open your heart to them, then you will be impacted negatively. You need to surround your heart with metal to protect your heart! Distance yourself emotionally! If they were to be taken away from you tomorrow, you would not feel for them; but you would feel your purpose to pass My Message was your only obligation that was taken away!"

TEACHING on "YOUR ONLY PERSONAL OBLIGATION IS TO ME!"

"You need to surround your heart with metal, for metal cannot be penetrable; but if you surround yourself with sponge, you will be soaked! You cannot take everything in, or make it personal. The only personal contact you have is Me! The only personal obligation you have is to Me! No one else is an obligation, but a choice! So, realize that you only have Me to answer to, and you only have The Father to obey! Harden your heart, and do not let them pierce through! You are working very hard to help and pass My Information, but you can only be used if you are alert and ready."

TEACHING on EQUAL PARTS LOVE, and EQUAL PARTS DISCIPLINE

"Equal parts love, and equal parts discipline is how you will maintain a happy household; for love is having My Presence, and acknowledging My Presence! To receive My Love, you are able to pass My Love on to others. To receive My Discipline and learn, you are able to teach the Wisdom it brings forth. Teach your household, and it will be merry. Scorn your household, and it will be empty. When they do not listen, just learn to love them and bless them. That is all I do with you!

"Even in anger, love expands! Remember to always use love. Even when I was angry, it was because My Love expanded for My Father's House and Kingdom! The purpose of anger is to tear down love."

TEACHING on SHARING YOUR FOOD: SOWING LOVE AND CARE (Ecclesiastes 11)

"I AM going to tell you a little story. Close your eyes and listen intently:

'It is summer time, and you have woken up. You are preparing breakfast, but you don't have any food to offer and prepare. On your way to the market, you meet people who have too much to carry; and they offer you parts of their groceries. By the time you reach the grocery store, you realize you have all you need to prepare the breakfast. By the time you reach home to prepare the meal, your house is full of people. If you don't measure the ingredients, you will not know how much food you will have to feed all the people. So, you conclude you have to make another trip back to the grocery.

'This time, you do not meet anyone; and you reach the store. On your way back, you meet many people walking to the store. You decide you have too much food, and offer it to them. By the time you reach home, you are left with only one bag of groceries. You realize that by the time you came to prepare the meal, you had no one left; because it was too late in the day. You enjoy your meal, but have plenty left over. When your plate is full, what do you do? Pass it on, of course.

'So, when your house is full again, you move your furnishings to accommodate the people and give them your food to eat. If one or two have questions on how you prepared the meal, your response is detailed; but if they continue to ask, your response shortens, and you lose patience.

'How many times have you asked, and asked; and how have I responded? Have I been short and impatient, or have I been gentle and patient? When you have plenty of food to prepare, give out and enjoy! Do not put barriers in front; for it is easier to share with a stranger, and accept from a stranger, than it is with people in your own dwelling!'

"So in this story, you learn to share by seeing how others have shared with you, and how you share with them; but most importantly, how you can move forward, and share at a later time without wasting your food! Sometimes you have too much food, and sometimes not enough; and sometimes you save it for later! You must now decide when you have too much, when you do not have enough and when you can save it for later. Do not become harsh! If you turn people away, then you double the work to bring them back! Burnt food never tastes or looks appealing!"

TEACHING on THE PROMISED MIRACLE

"I promised you a miracle, but you have not seen the miracle in front of you. Look back into your life: the changes are miraculous, you will notice! Let us rejoice in The Lord, and praise Him for His Patience, Love and Faithfulness!"

TEACHING on SHARING THE LORD'S BLESSINGS

"When The Lord blesses you, how do you express it? When The Lord blesses you, how do you share it? Most often, the blessing is too sacred to share with someone else; for only you will truly understand the blessing!"

TEACHING on MARRIAGE (1 Corinthians 7)

"Marriage is Holy! It is not a light omen, but a beautiful, blossoming Gift! During the duration of a marriage, the Gift will get rusty, dusty and dirty. It is up to you to maintain it, so it remains functional, shiny and clean.

"My People do not always see the same Light as I do. My People often make their own choices, and My People often get hurt and shaken. But in all this, I AM still their loving and gentle Father. It is important to be with My Chosen One, and not yours; for so many make this mistake, and realize it too late. However, as I have said, I can turn every single situation around for their good! An important tool to learn is forgiveness: to forgive, love and have patience to build is what you can take away from a bad experience.

"When your spouse will not understand or believe what is reality, it is not for you to judge. You can only be My Eyes, Ears, Mouth, etc. Your warnings will not go on deaf ears, for one day they will realize what you have been preaching. It may already be too late by that time, but that is not for you to judge. Judging is very easy to do, even when you are completely oblivious to it. My Judgment is only Mine to give! That day will come when I will judge, but it is not biased.

THE LAST MESSAGE

"Love your spouse heartily, as I love you. But continue to preach, teach and love them; for there is always hope of Salvation as long as they are alive. That is why it is important to choose wisely, and be sure it is with My Blessing; because it may be beautiful in the beginning, but it can easily rot at the end. Once you have already committed to your choice, to turn away is to break your commitment to Me; for when you made your choice, you committed to Me!

"I cannot separate what has been put together. Sometimes, the best blessings happen when you least expect them, in the 'worst' situations. You cannot do anything against your will, but your choices have implications. Only with a clean heart can you move forward. It is essential for My People to move forward with a clean heart, because you do not know when your time is up!

"I cannot grant the desire to stay away from the spouse of your choice, but I have given many brakes to follow-up on: the glue has to be dried before it is strong again! The basis of the relationship is the glue: it has to be strong again before you can consummate. Without the glue, it will fall apart! In order for you to resolve any issue, you must work on the glue. That is your key to unite or separate.

"Man lives on desire; but if there is no glue, the desire just remains a desire. It is man's sinful nature, which is natural for his wife; but only if it is mutual. Again, the glue! To create harmony, you must maintain the glue. Remember, the glue is what ties you together. The power of marriage is the glue! Once you solidify the glue, you can stand together; but without the glue, you fall apart. It takes time, effort, patience, love and forgiveness. Remember, I AM always around you. I AM always with you, and I AM always here! My Dear Beloved Children, what I promise you is peace!

"Even the smallest path goes is circles. Be sure to stay in circles. When one steers out of the circle, it leaves room for error. When a marriage circle is open still, and a person starts another circle, it leaves room for a lot of error by the enemy.

"Remember what I said: when you are one in heart, mind and spirit, you are one in body; but when you are not one in heart, mind and spirit, you cannot be one body! You see, this society sees it as one body and heart, but forgets that the mind and spirit play a huge role in maintaining the relationship. When you leave the body out of it, you can fix the heart, mind and spirit to be one; and then and only then can you bring the body to be one!

"That is why The Father detests fornication, for it blurs the mind, spirit and heart into thinking they are one. It blurs them from understanding the troubles, hardships and differences. The body is the enemy's power over you. The mind, heart and spirit are The Father's. Fornication destroys a relationship when the three are not one; but when the three are one, it is magical, and a Heavenly Gift!

"Your bodies belong to one another, and no one else. When wife and man unite, they belong to one another only. No one else except the husband is allowed to rule over the wife, and no one else except the wife is allowed to rule over the husband. You become one, but you are two individuals.

"There is the same similarity in My Relationship with you: you belong to Me, and I in turn belong to you! We are united in Love and Spirit, for I AM The Creator, and you are My Beloved! All My Children belong to Me, as I belong to all My Children. My Commandments are set to create peace and authority, for I AM the only Authority; but I have given you the same respect to have choice, to choose and to live with your choices."

TEACHING on WOMEN'S HEAD COVERINGS: (1 Corinthians 11)

"Head coverings are important, especially when you are in Church. Long hair is not enough for a covering. When you cover your head in My Home, you show your obedience and submission to Me! It is not necessary to cover your head all the time, for you are not in Church every minute.

"A head covering allows you to be protected from demonic attack; however, you do not require that form of protection all the time. In prayer, especially in deep prayer, it is recommended, for it gives you shelter; but it is not necessary. Even Mary did not cover her head all the time."

TEACHING on GIVING

"When I give, I give freely; but I know where the heart lies. When you give, do you know where the heart lies? Everyone is selfish when it comes to one thing or another. Is it up to you to judge what that selfishness is? Check the heart. Where is the heart and where is the heart heading to? Spending time with a person is the only way to discover where the heart truly lies. It takes time to understand where the heart lies!

"It is easy to bless; but if you do not know where the heart lies, then where is your blessing going to? The enemy eats up blessings if the heart is not pure; but if the heart is pure, then who are you to judge how the blessing is spent?"

TEACHING on TITHES and OFFERINGS

"What you should be considering is your friend's heart, not his decision to help others. It should be his concern to give to only those that have a heart for Me! The fact is, your friend loves; and his way of showing his love is to help financially. What you can do to help him is to purchase what he needs with the tithes, and the rest of his needs can be met by his own provision. The issue here is that his tithes are not going to someone who has a heart for Me! This way, you can teach him to help people who are in My Path, and not because they are blood-related."

TEACHING on "THE CONFESSIONS OF SAINT AUGUSTINE"

"You do not want to miss out seeing your reflection in the water! Whether you see a benefit to your reflection, good or bad, you still do not want to miss out on it. 'The Confessions of Saint Augustine', whether good or bad, will teach; you do not want to miss out on reading this book!"

TEACHING on "THE VULNERABLE ARE OPEN TO ALL STIMULI"

"When a person has vulnerability, it is the simplest occasion for the enemy to attack. Remember, the enemy controls the air; and that includes everything spoken and heard. Unless that person is My Follower, they are very open to all stimuli."

TEACHING on PROMISES

"Promise Me you will never stray away from My Word! This is now the second time. The third time, you will not come back! You must promise to never listen to the enemy, for what I say to you has been proven time and time again! For anything you need double-checking on, you must seek My Word! Understand this? My Word is the only Truth you will hear, or speak of, or attest to, or rely on: the only Truth comes from My Word!

"Let this be a lesson for you: if you choose Me, there is no going back. If you choose to turn your back on Me, then I wash My hands of you!"

<u>TEACHING on THE GOLDEN, ROYAL SHIELD of LIGHT</u>

"Say to yourselves: 'BY THE LIGHT SURROUNDING US, I AM SAFE, PROTECTED, LOVED, SHIELDED AND WHOLE.'

"Repeat after Me: 'THE SHIELD IS MY ARMOUR OF PROTECTION: I WILL NOT BE TOUCHED, I WILL NOT BE PENETRATED AND I WILL NOT BE WEAK! I AM STRONG IN MY FATHER, I AM BLESSED IN MY FATHER, AND I AM HALLOW OF SIN IN MY FATHER; FOR HE, THE FATHER, HAS WASHED MY SINS WITH THE GOLDEN, ROYAL SHIELD OF LIGHT.'"

By: ***"THE HOLY ONE"***

www.ingramcontent.com/pod-product-compliance
Lightning Source LLC
Chambersburg PA
CBHW030113100526
44591CB00009B/395